THE BEST GARDENING IDEAS FOR THE '80s

by the editors of
ORGANIC GARDENING®

TABLE of CONTENTS

Due to the effects of inflation, the reader should assume that the prices quoted throughout this booklet are generally low.

INTRODUCTION

Can there really be anything *new* in gardening?

The answer is YES. And in this booklet you'll find a wealth of great new gardening ideas for boosting production and making the most of your time, effort and money.

The past couple of years have been immensely progressive for organic gardeners. New discoveries in and out of science brought breakthroughs for increased production and better garden health. We've learned so much that's new, exciting and helpful that we put our 20 best stories together for you in this booklet.

Where did these fresh ideas come from? From new scientific research and from other gardeners whose trials and errors have led them to success. Now those years of effort are summarized for you to take advantage of.

The basics of gardening can be learned in one season. But the art of gardening takes a lifetime—or, as one longtime gardener has said, "I figure it'd take me at least three lifetimes to learn it all." While gardening in essence is simple, it is complex in its application due to the many variables involved: weather, sun, water, soil fertility, plant strain, etc. This booklet is the distilled wisdom of dozens of person-years of effort in dealing with these variables. You'll find no paint-by-numbers approach here. You will find practical recommendations built on deeper understanding of what's going on in the garden, the approach, to complete the metaphor, of the student who learns draftsmanship, composition and the proper use of paint.

Organic gardening, particularly, is a method that keeps growing naturally and undergoing subtle change and nuance. We learn, and we share with one another, techniques based on our understanding of nature. The more we understand, the more successful the techniques. And the more we understand, the closer our gardening approaches Nature's ways. We've seen that the more natural the garden, the healthier and more productive it is.

In contrast, chemical gardening tends to reduce the art of gardening to a set of dead rules. You don't need to know what's happening in the soil, in the insect kingdom, within the plant itself—just apply the right chemicals and let technology take it from there.

Organic gardening demands more from the gardener. He or she must know that an outbreak of pests means that something in

5

the natural checks and balances of the garden is out of whack. The job then is to penetrate to the core of the problem and settle things there, efficiently, intelligently, and as naturally as possible. Because in this way, the heading is more lasting and the garden becomes, again, more self-regulating.

We're excited about the discoveries and new techniques you'll find in this booklet. Many of us have used them with great success, and have read the letters of readers of ORGANIC GARDENING who've also found success using them. We think you'll find them easy to understand and use. What's as important, you'll find your own understanding of garden processes increasing and your abilities with vegetables keeping pace.

The Editors

HOW TO HARVEST ASPARAGUS ALL SUMMER LONG

YOU ARE ABOUT to get an education in the fine art of asparagus growing—how to handle the plant to get spears of optimum tenderness and how to double the length of the harvest season in most parts of the country.

What this means to you is that asparagus need no longer be a spring delicacy, whether cut fresh from the patch or bought stale at the store. For little more work than mulching each year, you can depend on it for meals through three seasons for decades to come.

Before learning how to grow it, we should decide just what we want from our asparagus patch. Because we're not growing it for market, we can trade some yield for succulence. Let's agree that for our tables, we want the tenderest spears possible.

Out at the Michigan Agricultural Research Station, scientists loaded a shear-press which measures the toughness of asparagus. "Results show that spear toughness increases with decreasing diameter and with increasing distance from the spear tip," they reported. And at Washington State University, scientists also found that "larger spears are more tender than smaller spears."

It was the number and diameter of the spears—not the difference between varieties—that affected tenderness the most. They further discovered that emerging spears were tougher following cold spells in the spring than when the weather was warmer. Finally, researchers at Michigan State University have just reported that "as the amount of rainfall increased during spear growth, the spears contained less fiber."

What we want then is big, thick spears. To that, let's add that we want them all summer long. Here's how to get them.

The first step is to choose your variety and decide whether you want to plant started roots or seed.

MARY WASHINGTON is the most widely grown and available variety, and it's tolerant to asparagus rust. WALTHAM WASHINGTON, FARIBO HYBRID, and MARTHA WASHINGTON are also rust tolerant although less widely available. These, along with RUTGERS

BEACON, are especially suited for gardens in the East and Midwest. The VIKING strain is recommended for gardeners in the most northerly parts of the country. For the West Coast, U. C. 157 and 500 W have been developed for the special climate there. Asparagus, which needs a dormant period caused either by freezing or drought, doesn't grow along the mild, wet gulf coast and Florida, but it will do fine in the mid-south, where PRINCEVILLE is the choice variety.

While gardeners have traditionally planted one-year-old roots, we're going to recommend starting your own plants from seed, for several important reasons. There's little chance of importing fusarium root rot on seed. Roots shipped through the mail or purchased from a store undergo a severe transplant shock. Your own plants should have a 100 percent "take" when set into the garden. Purchased roots may be either male or female plants. Females have a higher mortality rate and lower yields than males. If you allow your seedlings to bloom, you can mark the males and make your permanent bed entirely from these more vigorous plants. It's assumed that females are not as fruitful in terms of spears because part of their food reserves, stored in the fleshy

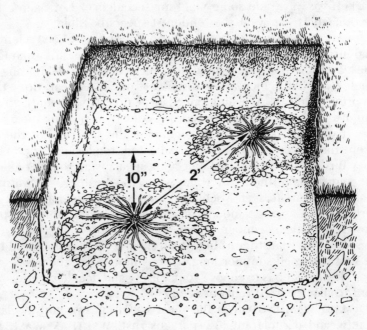

Deep planting (about 10 inches) gives the largest—and also the tenderest—spears.

roots, goes for berry production. Asparagus flowers are small, bell-shaped and yellowish-green. The male flower is larger and longer than the female, containing six well-developed stamens and a rudimentary pistil. The female flower has six rudimentary stamens and a three-lobed, well-developed pistil. A hand magnifying glass should quickly show you the difference.

In the first few years, crown-planted asparagus will make larger spears than directly seeded plants—but we don't take harvests the first couple of years anyway. Some asparagus-growing directions say to take light harvests the second year, but don't do it if you want large, tender spears in subsequent years. According to the USDA, "The crop must be grown for two full-growing seasons before harvest begins. This is necessary to allow the plants to develop an adequate storage root system to produce spears in coming years. *Any harvesting or damage to the ferns during the first two growing seasons dwarfs the plants and can reduce yield for the life of the bed.*"

After a few years, plants started from seed start outproducing those from roots, and continue to make slightly larger (and tenderer) spears for at least the balance of the 15 years that scientists compared crown and seed-planted asparagus.

Don't forget cost. A hundred roots will cost about $15 from a nursery. A hundred seeds will cost about 50 cents. Which leads us to consider how many plants we'll need for our garden. Figure on 40 crowns per adult. Planted two feet apart each way in double rows, two such rows of 40 feet each will be more than enough for a family of four. If 40 crowns per person seems like a lot, it is. It's double the recommended number found in almost all gardening publications. We're suggesting you plant twice the number because that is the key to all-season production.

We got the idea from Dr. Frank H. Takatori, a specialist in asparagus at the Department of Plant Sciences at the University of California, Riverside. "Here in Riverside, where more backyard asparagus is grown than anywhere else, I suspect," he said, "I encourage gardeners to plant double what they'll need. I tell them to harvest half the bed until early summer, then let it grow to fern. At that point, cut down the ferns that have grown on the unused half of the bed. That portion will send up spears that can be cut until cold weather slows production. The spring bed should be harvested in spring only, and the fall bed only in the fall." He explained that in most of the country, asparagus is limited to an eight-week cutting season because it needs the rest of the year to leaf out into ferns that manufacture the plant's food, which is stored

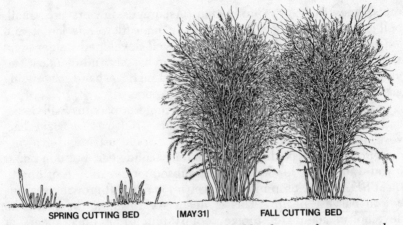

SPRING CUTTING BED   [MAY 31]   FALL CUTTING BED

To have asparagus all season, plant double the usual amount, then reserve half the bed for spring cutting only, half for fall cutting. When not being cut, the beds are allowed to grow to fern.

in the fleshy roots. Too long a cutting season means less time for food manufacture and storage, and tougher, thinner and fewer spears next year. A 12-week cutting season is recommended for California's gentle climate. An eight-week season is long enough for the Midwest and East—usually from early April through the first week in June. But in the bed for fall harvesting, food manufacture and storage goes on during the spring and early summer. Cut down the fall bed's ferns in late July and enjoy spears until October's frosts. Meanwhile, the spring bed has leafed out and is making food to produce next spring's bounty.

Say you've decided to start 100 seeds next spring. Plant them one to a peat pot in early March and make sure they get daily sun. They do best at temperatures from 60 to 70, which a sunny windowsill or a spot in the greenhouse will provide. Let them grow about 12 weeks, or until about 12 inches tall. Plant them 2 to 3 inches deep in a nursery bed if you're going to select the males, or right in the permanent bed if you don't mind the lower (by from 25 to 30 percent) production from a mixed-sex planting.

How asparagus beds are prepared and plants are set in has everything to do with the size of the spears produced.

First, choose the site carefully. The bed will be there for a long time. Most references put a bed's life expectancy at about 25 years, but I personally know of a bed 40 years old that's still

10

producing. The site should be in a well-drained area. Asparagus will die out quickly if its roots stand in water for even a few days.

It was mentioned that spears grow tougher after a cold snap in the spring, so if possible, plant the bed along a sunny south wall. If you have no wall, make sure the bed gets full spring sunlight. Some growers hasten soil warming by laying lengths of black plastic along either side of the bed in the spring. Sandy soil warms up more quickly than heavy soil, and it drains well, too, so that makes sand an important ingredient in the bed.

For double-row asparagus, dig a trench one foot deep and a little more than two feet wide. When replacing the soil later, you'll want to mix in a quarter sand and a quarter rich humus—like rotted manure, leaf mold or compost—with the ordinary soil from the trench. Asparagus likes a soil with a pH of 6.5, so if using leaf mold, check the pH and add ground limestone if the mixture is too acid. Compost tends toward a pH of 6.5 naturally.

Almost all popular garden directions say to loosen the soil and layer the bottom of the trench with rotted manure. But a check of what science knows about asparagus shows that it isn't necessary. "It's been found that asparagus roots are mostly lateral, and even grow upward from deep-planted crowns, and that the roots which do grow downward thrive in a more compact stratum," wrote one USDA scientist in a farmer's bulletin.

Five inches is the usual planting depth recommended for asparagus in the Midwest and East, eight inches or more for the sandy or peat soils of California. But in 1976, scientists at the University of Illinois planted crowns at five and 10 inches deep to see what effect varying depths would have on spear yield and thickness. They found that "the shallower plantings came into production a week earlier each year than the deeper plantings (perhaps an advantage for the deeper setting, since they emerge later into warmer air and that can mean tenderer spears). *While there were fewer spears from the deeper plantings, the individual spears were much larger and heavier,*" the researchers stated.

The trench is 12 inches deep and the plants should be set at 10 inches for later emergence of much larger spears. That leaves two inches to be made up. And that's done by making a mound in the bottom (ridging) over which the young plants' roots are spread. Many growers plant their crowns on the flat bottom of the trench, digging it only five to eight inches deep. Scientists at the Luddington Experimental Horticulture Station in England tested ridged- versus flat-planted roots in a five-year trial. They found that the total number of spears was 40 percent higher from the flat rows than from the ridged rows. *But,* they also found that almost 60 percent of the spears from the ridged rows were of the two largest grades, while only 35 percent of those from flat rows were in the premier grades. When they compared weights, *the ridged rows produced two and a half times the amount of sheer asparagus,* mostly because of the larger, thicker (although fewer) spears.

So, we recommend making a two-inch mound of soil in the bottom of the trench, which puts the planting depth at 10 inches—just perfect for the largest, tenderest cuttings.

A California test several years ago involved varying the distances between plants to see the effect on yields. Plants were

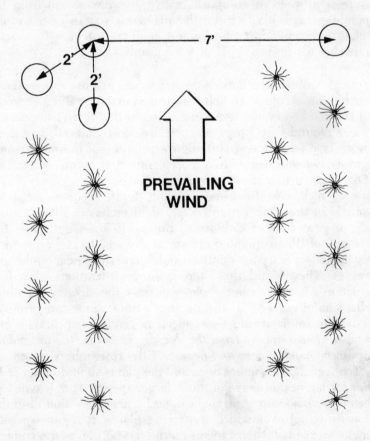

Planting tests show that crowns should be two feet apart in double rows seven feet apart for optimum spear size.

grown one foot, a foot and a half, two feet and three feet apart in rows seven feet apart. The results showed that *crowns two feet apart produced twice as many spears, and heavier spears*, than crowns spaced more closely. Planting them even farther apart didn't affect yields that much. This is understandable when we realize that in light soils, asparagus roots can grow to fill a six-foot circle, and that in heavy soils, roots can still reach a diameter of four feet. So, along with the 10-inch planting depth, we're recommending a spacing of two feet apart each way in double rows seven feet apart.

We say double rows because in a 1975 experiment reported in *California Agriculture*, "a significantly greater number of larger spears was obtained each season in the double-row plantings than in single rows. Our data show that the average spear size was reduced in plantings with more than two rows per bed."

Back at Luddington, another test by the asparagus researchers there compared spear number and size when cutting was stopped on June 8 and on July 8. They found that beds stopped on June 8 made more and larger spears in later years compared to beds cut until July 8. A June stop gives the spring bed about an eight-week cutting season, and allows plenty of food to be stored to produce the largest kind of spears in subsequent years. In the East and Midwest, the fall bed should also be kept to no more than 10 weeks—a longer time because the bed will taper down production as the weather turns colder.

In Europe, some gardeners prefer to mound dirt over their emerging spears to blanch them. Yet the practice may be harmful to the bed, according to a team of Australian scientists, who point out that "production of green spears rather than blanched ones may ensure greater yields in subsequent years because of the carbon-conserving ability of the green spear."

Let's pretend it's next June, and you have dug the trench, and mixed sand and rotted manure, leaf mold or compost into the excavation soil. You make ridges in the bottom and set in the crowns or the seedlings. Now cover the young plants only about two inches deep with the soil mixtu.e. Water well. Come back in a week or two and move another inch or two of soil into the trench to smother young weeds. Pinch off any low, emerging branches that might be covered as you add soil. Over the summer this procedure is repeated until all the soil has been moved into the trench and the soil is slightly mounded in the bed. It will settle over the coming winter. At this point mulch the bed with leaves, compost, rotted

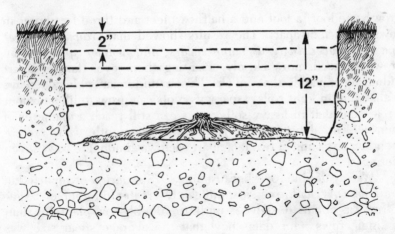

When setting out new crowns, two inches of soil every two weeks are moved into the trench.

manure or grass clippings. Don't let weeds take hold, as asparagus will respond to the competition by withholding yield and size from its spears. If you follow this planting procedure in the spring of 1980, your first harvest will be in the spring of 1982. In that first harvest year, pick spears only for two weeks. In 1983, you can increase the harvest season to four weeks, and in 1984, to the full eight weeks (in California, make that a 4-8-12-week succession).

The yearly additions of mulch, rotted manure or compost should be all the fertilization that light-feeding asparagus needs. Scientists have found, however, that the plant is very sensitive to zinc deficiencies in the soil. Under organic cultivation, with the use of manure and compost, zinc deficiencies are highly unlikely.

If you have an established asparagus bed that's been giving you lots of spindly spears, no matter how much organic nutrition you give them, the crowns may have grown too close to the soil surface. Crowns grow upward at about an inch per year, but heavy mulches also raise the surface. Here's a way to increase spear size. When the harvest season for your bed, whether spring or fall, is about half over, six inches of soil may be carefully ridged over the rows. This has the effect of increasing the depths of the crowns which, as we know, has the further effect of increasing spear size and enhancing tenderness.

There are some miscellaneous tips that would-be champion asparagus growers should be aware of. Since dry periods limit the growth of ferns, and thus of the food they can store to make next year's spears, you should water your beds deeply during any prolonged dry spells.

Where feasible, the rows should parallel the direction of the prevailing winds. The ferns thus support each other in winds and reduce chance of breakage and consequent setback to the plant.

After winter arrives and the ferns turn brown, don't remove them. They tend to hold the snow, providing extra ground cover and protection against deep freezing and thawing, which can injure the roots.

Another way crowns can be injured is by jabbing a knife into the soil to cut off spears. Unemerged portions of spears will likely be too tough to eat, and that knife could be injuring roots or spears just starting upwards. The proper way to harvest is to snap the spears off at ground level with the fingers.

Experienced growers know not to start an asparagus bed in an area recently used for strawberries. There is a virus that attacks strawberries and asparagus, and your planting could be wiped out.

That brings us to asparagus diseases and pests in general. These should be checked early, since insects can damage ferns' ability to store food—and if the damage occurs in the first few years, can permanently injure the bed.

Asparagus rust can be a problem in areas with wet growing seasons, such as in the East. Damage only becomes visible about midsummer, when rusty-brown spots break out on the stalk and branches of the plant. A light dusting of the plants with elemental sulfur dust about three weeks after cutting stops, and another a month after that, will control the rust.

The asparagus beetle is probably the worst pest of this crop. It has a curious design on its back, with white square patches against a dark background. It lays its dark eggs in rows along the fernlike leaves of the plant, and its larvae are a light gray or brown with black heads and feet. It and the 12-spotted asparagus beetle may be controlled by allowing several spears on either end of the bed to grow as a trap, then dusting the infestation with rotenone. If you are planning to grow a bed for fall cutting, look for the beetles and their larvae on that bed's ferns, which will be leafed out through the spring. There is another insect, the asparagus miner, which can sometimes be a problem. You'll notice zigzag miners on the stalks and branches. Tear out any infested ferns in late fall or in spring.

In most areas, organic gardeners shouldn't have much problem with these insects, as they have abundant natural predators that will be encouraged by your poisonless method.

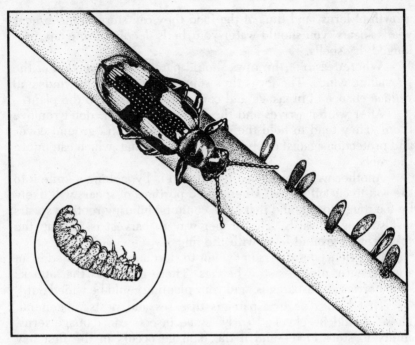

The asparagus beetle lays rows of slender black eggs on the ferns. Its larva (inset) has a black head and legs.

Besides great taste, what's in asparagus for our bodies? How do they rate nutritionally? The answer is that they are a very good source of several important food elements, especially thiamine, riboflavin, niacin, calcium, iron and vitamin C.

Perhaps the best thing about asparagus—the tastiest member of the lily family—is the fact that it is up to greet the returning spring before almost any other vegetable. Which means we're out early each spring to greet the asparagus!

JEFF COX

GARDEN BEDS SAVE TIME, WORK AND SPACE

The use of growing areas reduces the problems of soil compaction, giving you a more productive garden and less work.

GARDENS ARE CHANGING. All across the country, gardeners are rapidly putting to use a new type of gardening that disdains neat rows all lined up like little tin soldiers. These new-style gardens feature growing areas, the planting of four or five "rows" within one row.

The reason behind the shift in garden layout is simple. It's easier and more productive to garden in what are termed growing beds than it is to garden by the old-style row method. The new mode goes under many names, with each school of thought having its own unique methodology. Yet they all boil down to the same basic design of not planting in individual rows, but grouping your plantings together into blocks or beds anywhere from 18 inches to six feet wide.

Although gardeners' reasons for switching to beds are varied, the main benefit they all receive—whether they know it or not—is improved soil structure. While advocates of growing beds will point to the many advantages of beds, far and away the thing they do best is prevent soil compaction within a plant's root zone, allowing for optimum growth.

Dr. Albert Trouse of the USDA's National Tillage Machinery Laboratory points out that we now have bred specialized varieties for higher yields, and many people offer optimum fertilization to the plants, yet they grow them in compacted soil. "That's like taking a thoroughbred race horse for a pony ride. With proper soil structure and no compaction, you'll have a real racetrack for those hybrids to run on," he said.

"Wherever you have cultivated soil, it is vulnerable to plow pan," Trouse claimed. In a garden, undergoing constant cultivation, the potential is much greater.

A plow pan is formed by the compaction of finely pulverized (cultivated) soil particles into a thin, nearly impervious strata. This strata is a very effective barrier to root growth and to moisture travel. Plow pans form at the deepest level of cultivation, where pulverized particles get compressed against uncultivated soil.

Paths Lead to Most Compaction

Paths are the part of the garden subject to the most compaction, as they receive the most traffic. The overall effect of planting in beds is that the number of paths is decreased, as is the area of the garden subject to compaction. In a traditional garden, you have a small strip of planting area, the row, with wider bands of compacted soil on either side, the paths.

It doesn't take a genius to see that the side without traffic is far superior to the trafficked. In a garden of growing beds, the number of plants subjected to root-zone compaction is greatly reduced, as four or five rows of plants are put into one bed—instead of five rows flanked by six paths.

When talking about soil compaction in the garden, Dr. Trouse is quick to note that it doesn't take massive tractors to create plow pans. In studies in India and Poland of fields that have never been mechanically farmed, Dr. Trouse has found compaction problems as bad as he has seen on large mechanical farms in this country.

He explained that the more you cultivate soil, the more vulnerable to compaction it will be. "A well-cultivated garden soil may need as little as 3½ pounds of pressure per square inch to form a plow pan. People walking flat-footed create about 5½ pounds of pressure, more than enough for compaction," he pointed out. "When they get up on their toes, the balls of their feet, or their heels, the pressure goes up to 15 pounds, and you really have compaction," he added.

So what's a gardener to do? Dr. Trouse recommends that once you cultivate the growing area, stay completely off it. That's best done by using growing beds.

To see how detrimental a plow pan can be, let's assume you have a well-tilled garden, with a plow pan about one foot deep. The only water the plants can effectively use is what is in the area *above* the compaction. In a sandy soil, one cubic foot can generally hold about ½ inch of available water, while soil high in organic matter can hold as much as 1½ inches of water. Garden plants use an average of about 2/10 of an inch of water a day.

When you figure that plant roots can grow an average of 2½ inches a day, and the root systems of almost all plants can go as deep as six feet, you can calculate the amount of available water in an area without a plow pan, as compared to that with a plow pan. With a one-foot-deep plow pan, anywhere from ½ to 1½ inches of water would be available to the plant, or from three to seven days'

Once the permanent bed is constructed, walk no more on the growing areas! By avoiding compaction, you'll benefit from increased yields.

worth. However, if the plant can reach the entire six feet with its roots, you have a water supply that will last from 15 to 45 days.

With that information in mind, Dr. Trouse compared gardening with a plow pan to gardening in a window box. "If you have a one-foot-deep plow pan, a plant has only one foot of growing area, when it optimally could use up to six feet," he points out.

Dr. Trouse continued his explanation of the dangers of a plow pan by examining the effect of inadequate moisture and nutrients on a plant. "A plant will put out as many as 14,000 new feeder roots each day. It's up to these feeder roots to gather the water nutrients the plant needs. If the feeder roots are getting enough water and nutrients, the plant can operate at 100 percent and make maximum use of sunlight," he explained.

"However, if these roots cannot get enough water or nutrients, if they are restricted to a one-foot growing area, the plant will not operate at peak efficiency," he said. He emphasized that "this is well before any visual signs of wilting would set in."

The detrimental effect of a plow pan can reduce a plant's operating efficiency anywhere from 25 to 50 percent according to Dr. Trouse. "And you don't need the classic rock-hard plow pan to stop the growth of feeder roots," he added.

Getting Rid of Compacted Soil

Thus, the challenge is to decide if you do have a compaction problem in your garden, what to do about getting rid of it, and not cause another to form. Next time you get a good rain, wait three or four days, then go into the garden with a pointed metal rod. Slowly push the rod into the soil, and you will feel any levels of compaction before the rod hits the subsoil. The other option is to wait until the soil dries, and dig a soil profile from the surface to the subsoil.

If you find you have a plow pan, there are several things you can do. You can subsoil the area and plant a vigorous grass, then let it grow without any traffic on it for two or three years, and let the roots strengthen the soil to reduce future compaction worries. However, if you want to keep the garden area in production, you can break up the plow pan mechanically through deep cultivation. On farms, massive chisel plow-type equipment is pulled through fields with compaction problems. But in the garden, it normally must be done by hand or tiller.

One alternative is to sink a pickax or spading fork as deep as you can wherever you will be planting, as all you have to do is pierce the plow pan in the area below the plant. The other option is to either till or dig through the plow pan. Experiments at the Tillage Machinery Lab have shown that the L-shaped tines of a rotary tiller tend to spank the ground at the bottom of their stroke to form what Dr. Trouse considers "less than ideal conditions." On rotary tillers with the L part removed from the tine, leaving a straight knife effect, results were much better, reducing plow-pan formation.

Dr. Trouse cautions that "If you're not willing to change your cultural practices to prevent future compaction, don't subsoil. What man tries to improve upon is normally where all the trouble is." However, he added, "If you subsoil and then don't walk on the growing beds, you'll have a superior garden."

Although breaking up a plow pan may be hard work, preventing one is not. Simply put, plow pans are formed in the very shadow of cultivation. Meaning that if you walk or ride over the soil after you cultivate it, you will be forming small plow pans everywhere you step. The more you walk, the more complete and impervious this barrier becomes.

The solution is to mark off the areas you will be growing in, then stay off them and limit your movement to established paths. In the USDA's work, the establishment of permanent paths to control traffic in large fields is the main answer to compaction problems. Between the areas of compaction, growing beds are formed with very good soil structure where test yields have reached three times the national average. You can do the same in your garden by establishing permanent growing beds and permanent paths. If you can't establish permanent areas, be sure at least to stay off the growing beds once established each year.

More Benefits to Growing Beds

In addition to improvement in soil structure, growing beds offer a host of other advantages. By concentrating your water and fertilizing only on areas to be planted to crops, you'll average a 40-percent reduction in the amount of ground under care. Besides, the improved soil structure allows plants to use the water and nutrients you supply much more efficiently.

Perhaps the best-known advantage of a growing bed is what is termed a "living mulch." The concept is that by planting rows close together, as the plants mature, the leaves will overlap. That provides very good shade cover for the soil, both reducing water loss and greatly reducing weed-seed germination. If you've ever stood

21

in the middle of a mature forest on a hot summer day, you can appreciate this shading effect.

In a standard row garden, each and every plant stands alone in the row, with rows starkly separated from each other. With growing beds, the plants' foliage forms a much denser canopy. This increased leaf mass makes for much more efficient use of available solar energy. Dr. Eugene P. Odum, professor of zoology at the University of Georgia, has written that scientists have consistently found that maximum broadleaf crop production is achieved when the leaf surface equals four to five times the surface area of the garden. You cannot reach this level with standard row spacings.

What Odum's work means is that row gardens do not use all the solar energy that is available to plants. Compounding the problem of not using all the sunshine, plants standing alone use much more water than do those growing in a thick stand. Wind has a strong drying effect on both plants and soil. For example, a staked tomato plant that stands up in the air may need twice as much moisture as one allowed to run along the soil, due to increased transpiration when exposed to the wind. In a growing bed, only the two end rows would be exposed to the increased drying effects, while the middle rows would be well protected.

Another area of gardening that greatly favors growing beds is the idea of companion planting. In beds, the beneficial effects of mixed cropping are much more pronounced than in row gardens. With growing beds, short-season crops can be planted along with long-season crops in the same bed. The short-season varieties will benefit from the other crop, yet be harvested before crowding ever becomes a problem. Growing beds are ideal for combining companion planting with succession planting for maximum yields.

As your season starts to wind down, it is very easy to put small portable cold-frame-type devices over an entire growing bed to preserve your harvest longer into the year without wasting precious cold-frame space on paths. By making all your beds uniform in size, cold frames and shading devices will be completely interchangeable.

It's hard to understand how the tradition of individual rows got started, for horticulturists have long known that plants grow best when closely grouped. Almost all gardening throughout history has used some form of bed configuration, except in the last 70 to 80 years. Perhaps the shift from beds to rows was done to mimic large-scale agriculture as it shifted over to mechanical means of cultivation. How ironic that now the USDA is looking at large-scale use of growing beds for field crops, while gardeners are still using the row system.

Planting beds lend themselves to trickle irrigation systems. Water is piped to the entire bed at once, with feeder lines in the paths.

Plan a Bed Garden

To plan a bed garden, there are only a few things you must remember. First, don't make your beds too wide. You should be able to reach the middle of the bed from either side, so you won't have to walk on the soil.

To figure out plant spacings, just use the spacing given on the seed packet for plant distance within the row, and ignore the advice about how far apart to put the rows. If a head of lettuce can have additional heads growing 12 inches away from it to the north and south, it can also have heads 12 inches away from it to the east and west. By improving your soil structure and avoiding compaction, you will have more vertical root growth in place of horizontal root growth, allowing more plants to be closer together.

If you are gardening an area that has a soil-compacting problem, try to work the soil in the growing beds as deeply as you can, without disturbing the soil stratification too much. Again, once you have worked the soil, stay off it.

If you are preparing your garden with a tiller or a shovel, cultivate only the area you will be planting. Once the soil has been worked, gently rake the sides of the growing bed toward the middle, to give about six inches of sloped side on each side of the bed. If you cultivate an area four feet wide, you should have a planting space about three feet wide left. In this area you can plant as many rows of plants as you wish, or you can use a matrix planting pattern, using octagonal spacings instead of straight rows. But, for beginners, it's best to stick to rows—spaced closely together.

Some beds should be four feet wide, while others may only be wide enough to support a double row of a climbing or sprawling vegetable. Generally, the smaller the vegetable, the better it does in beds.

RAY WOLF

HOW TO KEEP VARMINTS OUT OF YOUR GARDEN

The backyard gardener's biggest problems are not blights and bugs, but birds and beasts. Here's how to cope—without going to war with them.

SCENE I: A warm May rain has fallen overnight and you go to the garden in the morning with a cheery whistle, knowing the corn will be peeking through the soil—faint green traces of row across the garden that promise platters of golden roasting ears in August. Instead, to your dismay, you find a hole pecked into the soil where every blade of corn should be. The birds, those lovely birds, have eaten every sprouted kernel in the patch. A hundred thousand cuss words will not bring a one back to life, but you try anyway.

SCENE II: Yesterday you set out cabbage plants, plants that you had carefully nurtured in peat pots in your cold frame so that there would be no transplanting shock. Overnight, nature helped out with a gentle rain. This morning you know the plants will be standing perky and straight and growing vigorously. You go to the garden and find instead that the cabbage plants have all disappeared, leaving only their poor little stumps behind. Yeah, that's right. That cute wild rabbit you let nest in the pachysandra has paid you a visit, and brought along Flopsy, Mopsy and the whole gang.

Almost every gardener must go through the pangs of a garden lost to wildlife at least once, but unfortunately many of us insist on going through it year after year because we believe there is an easy way out of the problem. We believe there is some magic folklore by which the wildlings can be frightened away. Maybe so, but over the years I have tried about every scare tactic known to keep wild birds and animals out of my garden. The list of those that have not worked reliably is two pages long. The list of those that *have* worked is two words long—*proper fencing.*

Scarecrows, shining strips of metal, aluminum disks, plastic owls, hoses entwined in trees to look like snakes, recordings of alarm in bird language, recordings of cussing gardeners, string stretching in crosshatches over the plants, blinking lights, explosions—none of it works for long. "Even deer become used to the scare devices which make loud noises at intervals," reports Jan Woelffer from Wisconsin. "After a while they keep on eating."

25

Nor is there any smell noxious enough to scare away animals either. Blood, blood meal, urine, dead animal carcasses, mothballs, gasoline, kerosene, creosote-soaked rags, or any commercial concoction of these folk remedies, work—if at all—only a short time. I used to be afraid to say that flat out in print, but now there's some scientific data to fall back on. Bruce Mays, in Illinois, reports that the University of Illinois has tested "a selection of as many rabbit repellents as they could think of" and not one of them worked.

"The researchers set out rows of cabbages in enclosures where the rabbits were penned," writes Mays, who had gone to the Extension Service searching for help against the rabbits that were eating up his garden. "One row in each of three enclosures was not treated. In the other rows plants were encircled with blood meal, with mothballs and with commercial blends. One row was lined with creosote-soaked paper. They set water jugs between plants, and coated others with chili powder. The rabbits were even fed their usual ration of pellets on the side. But the researchers reported that the cottontails ate every cabbage plant in sight. One researcher, Stan Reshesky, said he thought the rabbits particularly relished the plants coated with chili powder."

Put Plant Raiders on the Sauce

The only repellent we've been able to find some scientific support for is—hold your breath—Tabasco sauce. Jan Woelffer reports to us that Dr. Francis Gouin at the University of Maryland, College Park, has achieved a measure of success against mice, rabbits and deer with a mixture of one tablespoon of Tabasco sauce and one tablespoon of Vapo-Gard, a commercial adhesive agent, in a gallon of water. (The organic user can replace Vapo-Gard with ½ cup nondetergent soap.) There is some doubt, however, as to the long-standing effectiveness of this practice.

But the only sure way to protect your plants is with proper fencing and screening. Rabbits, probably the worst pest of all, are fortunately the easiest to fence out. Stake a chicken-wire fence (24-inch height is adequate and that allows you to step over easily) around the vegetables to be protected. You don't want the fence to be too flimsy, but neither do you have to stretch it super-tight or super-solid. I sharpen 3-foot pieces of 2x4 and drive them a foot into the ground for cornerposts, then use any handy sticks for posts every four feet between corners. The small steel or fiberglass electric posts are very handy for this purpose if you have them, since they are easy to insert and pull out of the ground. As long as the bottom of the fence is down against the soil surface and fairly tight, rabbits will not try to scoot underneath, Peter Cottontail to the contrary, and they don't jump over. Such a fence can be rolled up and unrolled, and moved around to various parts of the garden as the need arises without too much work.

For protection of fruit trees, wrap the trunks from soil level to at least two feet up, with either a commercial tree guard or a homemade type. I use a piece of metal window screen. In winter, tramp the snow down around trees so rabbits can't chew on low limbs. Wrapping tree trunks will not necessarily guard against mice—which can get below soil level and chew roots. Pull mulch away from trunks to discourage mice. Keep cats. Pray for owls.

A Shock for Groundhogs

All the other varmints that give you problems can either climb or burrow, and can be kept out effectively only with electric fence. Electric fencing is particularly effective against raccoons and groundhogs. Some gardeners get by with one wire about six inches off the ground, but two wires, the second another six inches above the first, are better. Use steel or fiberglass posts if possible, since coons have been known to climb wooden posts over the fence to avoid coming in contact with the wire.

Gardeners often assume that groundhogs will burrow under a wire, but these rodents seldom do unless their dens are very close to the garden. Most of their digging is confined to den sites, and when they journey for a meal to your garden they stay aboveground.

Squirrels and chipmunks can also be controlled with electric fence, though in these cases, you should erect a fine wire-mesh fence first, then run an electrified strand near the base on the outside and another near the top. Such an installation could become expensive, and squirrels and chipmunks are not usually destructive enough to warrant the outlay. But if your gooseberries or strawberries are mysteriously disappearing, you might check out that cute little chippy on top of your stone wall.

Penn State University is even working on an electric fence for deer made with the new high-tensile steel wire. But most gardeners in deer country do not think electric fence is practical against these high jumpers. "You need a permanent fence 10 feet high," says Woelffer. "That's expensive but worth it where deer are troublesome. An electric fence that high is not practical, and besides, deer too easily spook when jolted and tear up the fence."

A wire mesh cloche admits light, but not rabbits, to the lettuce patch.

Battling the Birds

Controlling birds, the bane of backyard fruit growers, requires a more serious commitment and investment in fences and screens. The plants have to be completely surrounded. That means, first of all, that the trees and bushes must be reasonably small— it is difficult to screen plants over about seven feet tall. Bush fruits and dwarf trees fit this category. "Even in sweet cherries, there are compact trees becoming available that are small enough to be protected practically from birds," says Robert Kurle a veteran backyard grower of unusual fruits near Chicago. "COMPACT STELLA and COMPACT LAMBERT are two experimental ones. GARDEN BING, a third, is available from Dave Wilson Nursery, 4306 Santa Fe

28

Ave., Hughson, California 95326. Stark Brothers plans to introduce a new compact sweet cherry, too."

A fine wire-mesh fencing makes a better screen than any fabric of plastic netting, and in any event, the latter can't be just draped over the dwarf tree or bush the way the advertising pictures show. Draping netting on a tree may save a few fruits, but birds will peck right through it. If you must drape, cheesecloth is a better deterrent than the wider-meshed fabrics.

However, the only reliable way to protect the plants is to build a screen box around them using stout, rot-resistant posts. Stretch

Inexpensive netting is especially appropriate for keeping birds from dwarf fruit trees.

and nail a fine-meshed wire fence around the posts. Nail 2x4 stretchers from post to post at the tops, and spread more fencing over the stretchers to form a roof. A screen door makes a handy entrance for you to get in and out.

An even better way to protect the plants is to make up 4-by-8-foot panels of wire mesh, using 1-by-4-inch boards for frames, and affix these panels to the posts and over the stretchers. The panels can be taken down and put up again after the fruiting season, then stored indoors the rest of the year. It will take time and money to build panels, but they should last a lifetime. Better to take care of four blueberry bushes in this painstaking way and eat your berries than to grow a dozen bushes without protection and eat none.

Keeping Feathered Friends from Corn and Wheat

But fencing will hardly solve the problem of birds eating sprouting corn unless you're rich enough to enclose the whole garden. The only type of enclosure I've found economical is to put plastic film over the corn, forming low tunnels over the rows. You can bend wires over the row and drape the film over these ribs like a miniature greenhouse, burying the edges of the plastic in the dirt along either side. Or you can use rigid plastic panels and hump them over the row with stakes on either side to hold them in a curved position. Neither way is practical for a large corn patch.

In a big corn patch, I use several stratagems, no one of which is entirely effective alone, but the combination has for two years proven satisfactory. First of all, I don't plant the earliest corn. The first extra-early corn is what the birds attack most greedily. Since there is only about a four-day period when the sprouting corn is relished by the birds, later corn—when there is lots of it sprouting fast in the neighborhood—is not badly harmed. (I'm prepared in any event to take a 10 percent loss and still harvest all we can eat.) Secondly, when I do plant corn, I plant a little oats with it. The oats germinate a day or so before the corn, but the birds do not seem to like oat sprouts. And for some reason, they don't seem to notice the corn sprouting and emerging right behind the oats—so most of the corn grows past the crucial time intact. Lastly, I cover the corn row after planting with an inch of composted chicken bedding. The mulch seems to confuse the birds as the corn emerges through it.

Some growers coat their seed corn with a mixture of tar and gasoline. I used to do that and cut losses from 50 percent to perhaps 25 percent. Since I now plant with a hand-pushed mechanical seeder, I can't use seed made gooey with tar or similar material.

If birds attack a garden patch of wheat you are growing for flour (a rare occurrence), the only thing you can do is cut the wheat, since it should be past the early milk stage if birds are showing interest. Put it on drying racks in a building that birds can't get into, and the grain will mature if cut in the late milk stage. If you grow yellow endosperm varieties of grain sorghum for flour, the birds may want their share too. The redder, bird-resistant varieties are the solution, though they are not quite as tasty.

Trapping birds and animals or shooting them is rarely effective. Adequate trapping is a skilled, full-time job, and even then by the time you bag the culprit, they will usually have done their harm anyway. *Never kill birds*, no matter how angry you get. Even starlings are beneficial to your bug-control efforts. Redwinged blackbirds are considered a common pest in the Midwest, and when I saw many of them in my Ohio garden a few years ago when the sprouting corn was being eaten, I stupidly shot a couple. Later I read that redwings eat many cutworms. I began watching them with binoculars. Sure enough, they patrolled the corn rows, but ate only bugs and worms. And though cutworm problems are common in our part of the country, we have never had an infestation.

Keep Your Temper

Don't lose your temper over shrews and moles either. Both do more good than harm. Moles make a lawn unsightly, but seldom do they harm your garden plants, even when they dig a tunnel right beside the row. Moles eat worms and grubs. Shrews eat mostly insects. Set your melons into plastic trays made by cutting gallon milk jars in half lengthwise. Put a hole in each tray for water to run out. The shrews for some reason don't like climbing into the tray to chew a hole in the melon.

Organically speaking, it is always better to fence than to kill because fencing harms no part of the biological food chain. Skunks will keep ground wasps under control. Rabbits are food for owls and hawks which control mice. In my strawberry patch I saw a large garter snake. After the first sudden fright and the irrational urge to kill that always comes in the aftermath of fright, I saluted the snake. Since garter snakes have occupied our gardens noticeably in the last few years, we have had no problems with slugs.

GENE LOGSDON

31

GLOBE ARTICHOKES – THE CALIFORNIA DELICACY THAT YOU CAN GROW ANYWHERE!

IF YOU'VE GOT 100 frost-free days in your gardening season, you can raise artichokes. Most of the country qualifies. But artichokes, one of the finest delicacies and a very nutritious vegetable, are virtually unknown as a garden crop outside of California, despite most gardeners' compulsion to beat all odds and grow the impossible. Three mistaken notions about how the artichoke plant grows are at the root of the problem. They have either caused failures in first attempts or kept people from even trying.

Myth 1: The artichoke must be grown as a perennial.

We have grown artichokes from seed at the Organic Gardening and Farming Research Center in Maxatawny, Pennsylvania, and harvested the first edible buds the same season—about the time the first tomatoes ripen. Farther north in the Berkshire mountains of western Massachusetts, Sherry Boutard has had much the same experience. The season there is shorter, but she's picked artichokes from seed-grown plants around the second week of August for three summers now. There's at least six weeks of harvesttime after that.

A lot of the credit goes to a superior variety, GRANDE BEURRE, which appears to produce fast budding plants in 50 to 80 percent of its seedlings. GREEN GLOBE, the commonest American variety, may produce *no* plants that form edible buds in the first season. GREEN GLOBE seedlings, therefore, must be kept alive through the winter, which sets the stage for another common failure.

In some ways artichokes are fairly cold-hardy. Their leaves can withstand frosts down to 28°F. In California, a frosty night or two slows winter bud production only slightly. But a freeze that penetrates into the soil will kill the crown and fleshy roots. Gardeners have tried to maintain them as perennials by covering the plants with a heavy mulch when the killing cold arrives. Even if freezing is warded off, rot starts to work under the mulch and digests the crown and all its dormant buds. Wherever the ground freezes, treating artichokes like a perennial involves a lot of work and a heavy risk of failure. There's no need to take those chances, as you'll see later in the article.

Myth 2: Artichokes can't tolerate intense heat.

The plant wilts very severely under intense sunlight, even when the ground is loaded with moisture. It looks bad for a while, but so do squash or cucumber leaves on any hot, sunny day. They recover later—and so do artichokes. Heat doesn't affect the health of the plant, but it can ruin the eating quality of the buds. They develop quickly then and tend to be small and tough. When the weather cools, though, the plant will start producing high quality artichokes.

Dr. Vincent Rubatzky, who knows more about the ways of artichokes than nearly anyone else in California, says there is no reason why artichokes can't be grown across much of the southern half of the United States, as long as the plants get all the water they need. The heart of large-scale artichoke cultivation, Dr. Rubatzky says, used to be in Louisiana.

During the intense southern summer, the plants should be kept trimmed back a bit to reduce water losses and inhibit bud-stalk formation. Stalks that are producing inedible buds should be cut out near ground level. Then about 100 days before the return of daytime highs in the 70's, the plants should be encouraged to grow. The fall harvest should be long. And where winter freezing is rare, the plants will also produce heavy spring crops in most years.

Myth 3: Artichokes are well adapted only to the California coastal zone, where winters are mild and summers are consistently cool.

It's far easier to raise high quality artichoke buds on the California coast than in any other spot around the country. The climate there is particularly suited to their needs, and artichokes can be harvested in every month of the year, though most farmers stop production through the summer. California is perfect for the *gardener* growing artichokes. But the *plant* probably couldn't survive there on its own. The climate is so humid that its seed rots when it hits the ground.

The point is that the plant is suited to a much wider range of climates than most gardeners believe. The artichoke much prefers the drier weather in its native country, the Mediterranean basin and particularly the coast of Italy. Winters there are colder than in coastal California, and the summers are much longer and hotter. The odds are good that if you've got 100 days of good growing weather, you can put together all the conditions necessary for homegrown artichokes.

In short-season regions, the best way to start is from seed, and all the first year successes we know have been with GRANDE BEURRE (Thompson and Morgan). Cultivated artichokes are only a generation or two removed from the weedy thistles common all over the Mediterranean basin. Many of the seeds from the finest plants will produce weed-like offspring. Some will flower late, and the buds of some will be tough and coarse. For centuries, artichokes have been propagated almost entirely by dividing good plants. California growers never use seed. But GRANDE BEURRE seems to be an exceptionally well developed and consistant strain.

When you begin with artichokes from seed, you are on the road to selecting your own improved strain. Of course, you could start fresh from seed each year. But it would be better to mark those plants that produce the earliest and nicest buds and save them for next year. The bare roots can be stored quite safely over winter in root cellar conditions. Or better, dig them in fall and hold them till spring in pots. Plants that can draw on the reserves of a healthy root will be more vigorous than seed-grown plants. Moreover, *all* of the ones you replant in the second season will be productive.

There are gardeners in California who have developed their own strains of artichokes after years of dividing only their choicest plants and trading or begging for root pieces of even better ones. If you know someone who raises excellent artichokes well enough to ask for a shoot or two, that is the best way to begin. But most of us aren't that lucky.

In hopes of getting bigger plants the first year, you could also buy dormant roots from California nurseries. All of them would bear good (though not necessarily great) buds, but you risk growing some that would mature quite late. Unlike gardeners, commercial growers in California do not rigorously improve their stock. When a field is dug for renovation, the poorer root pieces are thrown in the same bin with the best. Where the growing season is long and easy, it's nice to have some plants peaking early and others coming on later. But if you're racing bad weather, you want plants that mature on time.

Plan to start artichoke seeds at the same time you plant your first vegetable seeds indoors. To break dormancy, store the artichoke seed in the refrigerator in moist peat moss for two weeks ahead of time. Use bottom heat for quick germination. The artichoke seedlings should be transferred to individual containers soon

34

after germination, because the plant quickly begins to grow a long deep root. Don't set the plants out unprotected until all danger of frost has passed. If you use cloches or other protective devices, you can set them out two weeks earlier.

An artichoke plant demands a lot of space in the garden, and the soil must be fertile and well drained. Where the growing season is long, the plants can grow at least three feet high and four feet across. You'll need a row 25 feet long for half a dozen plants. Where the season is short, artichokes grow only two feet tall and two to three feet across. But since production is lower you'll need about a dozen plants to make a good harvest for a small family.

Artichokes are tenderest when they are encouraged to grow fast. That means rich soil and prompt watering whenever the soil dries. If you apply generous amounts of manure or compost to your garden each year, it should be in good shape to start artichokes. Set each plant into a 12-by-12-inch hole that is also filled with compost. If the garden is not manured, work four to five pounds of manure (a little more of compost) into the soil around each plant shortly after planting. Artichokes like the soil pH at 6.0, which is slightly acid.

Be prepared to provide regular supplementary feedings throughout the growing season for best production. This is doubly important when the plant will be getting frequent irrigation. At monthly intervals, side-dress each plant with blood meal, cottonseed meal or some other high-nitrogen fertilizer. Or use a manure or fish-emulsion tea. Fish emulsion is especially good because it is high in calcium, which is the one nutrient after nitrogen that will most severely restrict artichoke growth when in short supply. Growers in England try to make a special seaweed compost for artichokes whenever possible.

An artichoke plant must never be short of water when you are pushing it into production, especially when the temperature gets above 75 degrees. If your soil is heavy, plant the artichokes in a well-drained spot and consider working in some sand and organic matter to improve its moisture-holding characteristics.

In the South, where the plant may be ready to flower during unfavorably hot weather, you want to hold it back until about 100 days before the daytime high temperatures dip back into the mid 70's. Besides trimming back flower stalks and big leaves as needed, be very sparing of water during this period and withhold all supplemental feeding.

Mulch is an invaluable aid to artichoke culture. When the weather turns warm, the soil should be covered with a thick mulch of an organic material. This will insulate and cool the soil, reflect light from it and hold moisture in. After the weather is cool, remove most of the mulch. Some is needed to prevent erosion, but you want to let sunlight hit the ground and warm it.

Large size has little to do with good eating qualities in artichoke buds. Prime buds can range from two to five inches across. A perfect artichoke is one with the bud scales still lying tight and flat. When they begin to point out, the tenderest stage has passed. The stem of a perfect bud for eating should be soft and pliable for two to three inches below the bud. Cut each bud with about two inches of stem for a handle.

Artichoke plants become overgrown with the years. Old plants need to be constantly replaced with new plants to maintain steady production. Some growers do this every three years, while others keep the plants producing for six or seven years. To renew a bed every four years, for example, one-fourth of the planting should be replaced each year.

The best way to do this is with suckers or sideshoots taken from the best plants. Artichokes continuously grow new sideshoots, and they can be taken from the plant for propagation at any season. Suckers removed early will be strongest when the season comes to a close, while suckers taken after the dog days run less risk of succumbing to heat and dehydration.

The best size shoot for propagation has a piece of root with it that is two and a half to three inches long and at least an inch thick. Carefully dig around the base of a likely looking sideshoot. If it has a good-sized piece of root with it, cut it gently away from the parent, saving as many rootlets as possible. Trim off all the large leaves, keeping only one or two small leaves that will be protected by the stalks of the leaves you have cut away. Plant it right away, water it often and shade it a bit, if necessary.

Anywhere that deep-ground freezes are a threat, artichoke roots should be dug and stored indoors, because the crowns are very likely to rot under mulch. The roots can be safely stored for a long time if they are kept in a fairly dry place that is maintained between 33 and 40 degrees. The leaves should be cut back to within an inch or so of the crown and the roots carefully dug and brushed clean. They should be kept loosely packed in fiber bags (don't use plastic) or on a shelf. An even surer way of keeping them is to plant each one in a large pot. Put the pots in a cool, bright place. The crowns will immediately begin to regrow, but do not feed them and water very sparingly until shortly before the time comes to set them out in spring.

Where winters are not so severe but still bring freezes, gardeners have developed various ways of carrying artichokes through the cold out-of-doors. The simplest method is appropriate for mild climates. After the first killing frost, the large, damaged leaves are cut off, but the stems (at times tied together) are left to protect the crown and the growing point from the earth that is hilled up generously around each plant. No dirt is allowed to get into the center. Where it's colder, the trimmed-back plants are first covered with a wooden box, then the boxes are covered with a heavy blanket of earth and mulch. Where there are prolonged heavy freezes, some gardeners pile sifted ashes one foot deep over each trimmed plant. Any extra protection goes over the ashes, which apparently prevent decay. In 1916, horticulturists at the Geneva, New York, experiment station successfully carried about 50 artichokes through several winters by mounding each plant with a foot of coal ashes. Manure or compost almost always rots the plants.

The protective coverings should be removed promptly when all danger of ground freezing has passed. There is a danger, if the plants are protected too long, that shoots will start up too early. Those will be tender and very vulnerable to light spring frosts. But after the ground outside has thawed and the chance of a penetrating frost is over, take off all the mulch. Then the plant should come out of its dormancy very slowly, matched to the weather. Use cloches if heavy frosts threaten young leaves later in the spring.

There's more than one way to get an artichoke through the winter. Once you've started, and reveled in those delicious home-grown buds, you'll find the way that best suits your way of working and your climate. And if all the ways seem like too much, you can always start fresh from seed each spring. But, artichokes are no tougher to keep going in your garden than geraniums, dahlias or Belgian endive—once you know the tricks that work for each one. And to my taste, few vegetables can match artichokes for good eating or the chance to show off (at least to oneself) the riches with which a garden repays a little effort.

JACK RUTTLE

NEW VARIETIES FOR YOUR BEST GARDEN EVER!

Trigger an exciting year of home-garden production by grow-ing some remarkable new vegetables, fruits and flowers.

THE BIGGEST PLANT NEWS for 1979 has been made by a surprising new vegetable—the snap pea. It's an All-America Selections top award-winner, and actually a plant-breeding achievement that could make growing peas as popular as tomatoes. Called SUGAR SNAP, the variety belongs to a completely new family—unlike any existing type of garden pea or edible-podded pea. In growth and appearance, the snap pea looks like its regular garden cousin, growing full, thick pods. But garden peas must be shelled because the pods themselves are too fibrous and can't be eaten. Snow peas or the usual edible-podded peas, on the other hand, have flat pods and tiny peas, and they must be harvested at a critical stage or they'll grow stringy and bitter. SUGAR SNAP, how-ever, produces both fat, juicy edible peas and plump edible pods. The result is a pea that's more like a snap bean—but earlier, sweeter-tasting and more productive.

Dr. Calvin Lamborn developed the snap pea in a breeding program in Idaho, when a once-in-a-million mutation was found in a crop of regular garden peas. Dr. Lamborn had been trying to breed an edible-podded pea for some time, and was about to give up when the maverick specimen with twice-as-thick pod walls and extra-sweet peas appeared. Making careful crossing selections with it, he produced the thick-walled edible garden pea that maintains good quality. "When the pod is bent, it will snap like a fresh snap bean pod," he explains, "hence we are calling them snap peas."

Vegetable experts across the United States who've tried SUGAR SNAP agree that it promises to raise the popularity of garden peas by increasing the yield of edible matter. You end up with more than twice as much food per foot of row than from peas that have to be shelled. At the Organic Gardening Experimental Farm, snap peas grown in trial plantings over the past three seasons have produced very well. Editor Robert Rodale, an AAS judge for two years, says of the gold-medal winner, "It takes a popular vegetable and puts it into an entirely new category. We grew them in profusion, and found the yield, quality and flavor excellent. There's more to enjoy—not like the 'deflated balloon' effect of ordinary snow peas."

Unlike flat-podded sugar or snow peas which should be eaten when small, SUGAR SNAP remains in prime condition for days. The

A completely new vegetable, "Sugar Snap" forms full sweet peas in crisp, edible pods.

pods have a distinct appearance and flavor. Round (cross-section) pods with thick walls can be eaten at fully mature sizes, 2½ to 3 inches in length. Mature pods require stringing which can be accomplished quickly and conveniently while you are snapping the pods into bite-size pieces. The new snap pea is so sweet you can eat it raw, experiencing a crisp, clean flavor produced by the pods, and a juicy sweet taste produced by the peas. They are excellent as a cooked vegetable, requiring very little time, just light steaming or stir-frying to produce a buttery flavor. They're also easy to freeze for winter eating, although unsuitable for canning since the high temperature needed destroys the pod structure. Fresh or cooked, the crunchy peas-'n-pods are nicely filling, contribute fiber, vitamins and some carbohydrates, but not as much of the latter or of fats as shelled peas.

SUGAR SNAP has the same hardiness as regular garden peas. Seed can be sown directly into the garden after St. Patrick's Day over most of the United States. Plants grow quickly and are not bothered by frosts. They produce tall vines which are best grown up supports such as a short trellis or chicken wire. Pods are ready for picking in 70 days, and continue cropping until hot weather sets in. The new variety is being carried by nearly every seed company, and looks like it is about to become the best-received award-winner since the AAS started in 1932.

More New Vegetables

Several more All-America choices share the limelight, including vegetables of special interest to organic home gardeners. GRAND DUKE is a new kohlrabi, a plant that's making a comeback, thanks to intensive methods which demand compact plants that can produce lots of edible food per square foot. (If kohlrabi sounds odd to you, it's really a valuable root crop, an ancient cabbage-family member grown for its swollen stems which resemble aboveground turnips.) "Bulbs" of GRAND DUKE can be sliced for dips, grated for salads or diced for cooking like turnips. It's mild and sweet-tasting, and you can cook up the vitamin-rich inner leaves that taste much like kale or collards. A good-flavored hybrid, the silver-medal winner was bred for quick maturity, ready in only 45 to 50 days.

DUTCH TREAT, an All-America sweet yellow pepper, lets you know when it's ready to eat. Yellow fruits turn scarlet, then deep red before other varieties mature, growing sweet and thick-fleshed as they ripen. Bred in Holland, it clusters 5 or 6 peppers, each 3 to 6 inches long and shaped like dunce caps, straight up atop 12-to-

15-inch-tall plants. A multipurpose vegetable, it adds crunch, color and vitamins to salads, stuffed peppers and many other dishes.

SALADIN cucumber has resistance to all four troublesome infections—mosaic virus, scab, powdery mildew and bacterial wilt—built into its breeding. The AAS bronze medalist, ready in 55 days from seed, has vigorous vines that readily run up strings, fences or trellises to save space. SALADIN's main appeal is a nonbitter skin gene in its inheritance. Crosscut cukes, bright-green tender skin and all, make good eating. Fruit is medium-short, starting at 4 to 5 inches for pickling; seeds are small and develop slowly.

Two new winter storage squash varieties round out the '79 All-America vegetables. EARLY BUTTERNUT, which bears 3½-pound fruits just right for baked-dinner serving, is ready for picking and storing up to 10 days earlier than standard Butternut types. It has a tan flesh, light flavor and firm texture, along with seeds that can be dried and roasted. SWEET MAMA earned an AAS medal for early maturity (85 to 95 days), high production, and good flavor-texture quality. Averaging 2 to 3 pounds, the fruit has tolerance to fusarium wilt and squash borer damage, and the hard-shelled squash will keep well for up to 4 months.

An unusual striped tomato, the TIGERELLA, is one of 34 new vegetables introduced by Stokes Seeds. Maturing in just 55 days, the novel early tomato alternates red with orange stripes on 2-inch-diameter fruit. EARLY CASCADE produces clusters of 7 to 9 small-fruited 4-ounce tomatoes all season, starting in 52 days from seed. CRIMSONVEE is a Canadian-developed paste tomato with strong disease resistance and a concentrated set of thick-walled, crack-resistant, medium-sized fruit. Other Stokes newcomers include WHITE SUNGOLD, a white sweet corn maturing larger ears and yields 3 weeks earlier than SILVER QUEEN; BLUE HEAVEN squash with good tolerance to yellows, a blue-green exterior and snow-white interior; and two miniature or baby carrots, AMSTEL, already popular in Europe, and BABY ORANGE, both with smooth, bright-orange roots.

Harris Seeds, observing its 100th year, has a quartet of noteworthy introductions. DEEP RED lettuce, a loose-leaf, slow-bolting type, grows well in spring, fall and hot weather. Clusters of crisp curly leaves are deep, glossy green, tinged with intense red. WARRIOR beet, an improved University of Wisconsin hybrid, has quick, uniform growth, stays unusually smooth with a rich interior color and practically no zoning. It's very good for freezing, too. QUICKSILVER, a Harris development that's helping the comeback of white corn popularity, has excellent quality and yields, is adapted for early planting, and is ready nearly 3 weeks earlier than the rival SILVER QUEEN. SWEET SAL, a bicolor sweet corn maturing in mid-season, has an attractive mix of white and yellow kernels, better tip-fill, texture and taste.

Better Beans and a Prime Potato Prospect

One good way to make your garden the best ever is to add some beans, a vegetable family that scores high for important food values, productivity, usefulness and storage advantages. WHITE DUTCH, a 90-day runner pole bean, comes from the Vermont Bean Seed Company. It's a variety that performs well in hot, dry climates as well as other sectors, and a bean that's resistant to common mosaic and rust. Related to the lima bean family, WHITE DUTCH grows over 10 feet tall, sets 4 large seeds per 6-inch pod in a creamy-white to pole-green shade. It can be harvested as a fresh shell bean or dried.

ORIENT EXPRESS is a new extra-early strain of yard-long beans, sometimes called asparagus beans, available from Thompson & Morgan. A food staple in the Far East, yard-long stringless pods are red, need poles for support, and usually grow up to 2 feet in length. (They taste best at about 15 inches.) The new variety produces 2 weeks earlier, making good yields possible in cooler or shorter-season areas.

WILKIN is an edible soybean that Rob Johnston at Johnny's Selected Seeds considers the best in their trials over many years. Tall plants (over 2 feet) have excellent resistance to lodging, he reports, and yields have run 30 percent over FISKEBY V and ALBION on their Maine test farm. It's dependable in adverse weather, he adds, yielding uniform all-yellow small beans of fine quality.

Johnny's is also making seed available of the earliest-maturing grain amaranth from the Rodale Research Center at Maxatawny. SCARLET KEEPER is a late fall-harvest storage carrot, 7 to 8 inches long, that retains good cooking quality over winter. BIG BULLY is a new early-maturing (79 days) watermelon for northern gardeners who want a large fruit (15 pounds-plus). WHIPPER-SNAPPER, one of the earliest (52 days) compact cherry tomatoes, produces up to 100 inch-sized oval fruits with a just-right balance of sugars and acids.

Other introductions from Thompson & Morgan, the British seedsmen founded in 1855, include MUNCHEN BIER, an unusual edible-podded radish for above and belowground food; BIG BERTHA, a 72-day giant-sized sweet bell pepper, one of which makes a full meal when stuffed; a round 60-day zucchini called APPLE

"Grand Duke" kohlrabi, an All-America award-winner, is boosting popularity of this valuable root crop.

SQUASH that's good eating raw; and LONG WHITE, a slender, sweet white-skinned cucumber.

There's a new potato of special interest to ORGANIC GARDENING readers because it's reported to be remarkably higher in two significant food values—vitamin C and protein. For the past three years, Dr. Joseph Pavek has been working at the University of Idaho Research Extension Station in Aberdeen to breed the BUTTE variety, an improved strain of RUSSET BURBANK and NORGOLD. His efforts centered on developing a smoother potato, easier to grow and better yielding than its parentage. A "surprising plus," though, Dr. Pavek told O.G., was discovering that the new strain contains 50 percent more vitamin C ("actually 56 percent in some tests") and 15 percent more protein. That makes quite a nutritional bonus with a good growing variety. Seed of BUTTE is available from the Idaho Crop Improvement Association, Box 188, Idaho Falls, Idaho 83401. Mail-order and other seed firms will likely have the variety available for sale in 1980.

Burpee Seeds, longtime favorites of many home gardeners, has a new cantaloupe of note—the SWEET 'N EARLY that's ripe in just 75 days from seed sowing. The hybrid grows round to slightly oval 4½-inch melons with corky ribbing and a sweet, thick bright-salmon flesh. Besides producing so soon, SWEET 'N EARLY keeps bearing fruit long after other strains. Burpee trials showed it the longest-producing melon. Vines are resistant to powdery mildew.

Two watermelons and a honeydew top the introductions from Henry Field Seed & Nursery Company. KENGARDEN is a bush-type melon that grows like bush summer squash, producing high-sugar-content fruits about 12 pounds each, with small seeds. YEL-LOW DOLL has a crisp, sweet watermelon flavor with attractive yellow flesh. It matures early, with icebox-size fruits ranging from 5 to 8 pounds. EARLI-DEW muskmelon is a honeydew with that extra-sweet green flesh that makes this fruit popular. Resistant to fusarium wilt, it matures round 4-to-6-pound melons early in the season.

Park Seed Company, flower and vegetable specialists at it since 1868, have bred the SWEET BANANA WHOPPER, the first hybrid in sweet banana peppers. The 65-day variety grows faster, more vigorously and bears larger, thicker-walled fruits longer. GREEN WHOPPER is a zucchini-type squash with solid, dark-green fruits that have an appetizing sheen and fine flavor. Smooth, cylindrical fruits take 48 days to mature, then bear heavily over a long period. GOLDIE is a Park dwarf tomato, a 14-inch plant that fits neatly into hanging baskets, pots, and window boxes. Ornamental as well as productive, it yields round 1-inch golden fruit with a good tomato flavor, and bears the entire summer.

BIG MOON pumpkin, from Gurney Seed Company, is a mammoth type bred for folks who want to enter contests or put up all their pumpkin pies for the year at one time. It's reputed to tip the

A winter storage squash, "Sweet Mama" won 1979 AAS medal for early maturity, resistance to pests and disease, plus good eating quality.

scales at about 200 pounds or more. Gurney also has a new field corn called MISSOURI PIPE, which produces huge cobs just right for that old corncob.

One more vegetable organic gardeners may welcome news about is a new sweet corn, FLORIDA STAYSWEET, a hybrid developed at the University of Florida. Consumer taste-tests rate it superior, and the sugar content higher than existing strains is retained long after harvest—in fact after 10 days refrigeration it held three times as much as other varieties. A major advantage for O.G. growers is that it has excellent husk cover, which prevents insect damage to the ear. Illinois Foundation Seeds, Inc. (Box 722, Champaign, Illinois 61820) has the variety.

New Fruit Varieties Add to Menu

A bowlful of fresh homegrown fruit adds an indispensable ingredient to the family's food enjoyment. Garden-picked fruit also goes into cold cellars, preserves, frozen desserts, pies and other stockpiled supplies for off-season eating and nutrition. The new year's varieties can help get your yard producing more fruit.

For example, three tree fruits bred for the Dave Wilson Nursery by Floyd Zaiger have low chilling requirements, setting good crops in mild winter climates. These include DESERT DAWN nectarine, a highly colored, early-maturing variety; MID-PRIDE, a juicy, yellow-fleshed freestone peach ripening in July; and AUGUST PRIDE, a similar peach ripening in August. Wilson also has GOLD KIST apricot, EARLY SWEET nectarine, and EARLY GLORY peach, a trio of early-ripening stone fruits which turn out much sweeter and juicier than first-of-the-season crops normally do. AMBASSADOR, a hardy English walnut that bears nuts its first season, is another introduction. Wilson notes interest also in their two plum-apricot crosses, PLUM PARFAIT and SPRING RUBY, freestones which mingle the traits of both fruits, plus the 20TH CENTURY pear-apple, a sweet Asian pear that has apple crispness.

Strawberries stay up front as the most popular home-garden fruit, and two new varieties from W. F. Allen Company, berry leaders since 1885, make them easier than ever. DELITE, a late harvest choice, was developed at Southern Illinois University and produces well from Missouri east to Maryland. It is highly resistant to red stele and verticillium wilt—the two worst strawberry diseases—and also resistant to leaf spot, blight and scorch. For an extended gardening season, or for pick-your-own operations, its large, firm fruit and dessert quality are advantages along with the strong disease-resistance. EARLIGLOW, a high-yielding early-season variety, is also very resistant to the major strawberry diseases. Medium-sized deep-red berries have been especially productive in Ohio, Pennsylvania, Michigan, New Jersey, Maryland and Missouri.

Allen also introduces a new red raspberry and a thornless blackberry. SOUTHLAND, released by the N.C.-USDA breeding program, produces a summer crop of firm, bright-red berries, followed by an August-September crop. The plants are vigorous and can be maintained virus-free for many years without spraying, because the aphid vector that spreads raspberry viruses does not like to feed on SOUTHLAND. Because of its tolerance to varying climatic conditions and its freedom from virus diseases, it makes a good choice for any home-garden area except those near the Canadian border. BLACK SATIN, the new thornless blackberry, matures large fruit 7 to 10 days before THORNFREE, the first of the USDA's improved varieties. Plants are reported exceptionally vigorous and yields have hit 18,000 to 24,000 pounds per acre.

Stark Bro's Nurseries, reliable fruit-tree suppliers to gardeners for many years, introduces STARK EARLY LORING, a large freestone peach that ripens 10 to 14 days before LORING. Discovered in 1965, the variety has been tested and propagated since then, and shows it can take varying cold-winter periods more consistently. Besides big showy flowers it produces large round, yellow-fleshed freestone fruit that achieves an 80 percent overall red color well in advance of the date at which it would soften.

LIBERTY, a new apple recently named by the New York State Fruit Testing Cooperative Association has some valuable characteristics for the backyard fruit grower. Not only is it resistant to apple scab—the most devastating disease attacking apples—but it also shows a high degree of resistance to three other major diseases—cedar apple rust, fire blight, and mildew.

Two apple varieties developed in Israel are being recommended for growing in Florida. ANNA, similar to the RED DELICIOUS and EIN SHEMER, a larger yellow type, fruit well in the central zone as far as north of West Palm Beach. Ogden Nursery Products has the tree stock, which ripens in the second or third year with less chilling requirements than northern types.

An innovation in blueberries is the dwarf TOP HAT, introduced by Dean Foster Nurseries, small fruit specialists since 1837. It's a true miniature, with an attractive "bonsai" look and small leaves but regular-sized berries. The self-pollinating plants, growing to about 14 inches high, are covered with fruit. The indoor-outdoor TOP HAT makes an interesting new choice for potted plants, hanging baskets and patio containers.

New Flowers Brighten Gardens

Flowers too? You bet. The world would be drab indeed without nature's alluring "food for the soul."

Among ornamental All-America Selections for 1979 are a pair of giant zinnias, PETER PAN GOLD and GOLD SUN, both colorful bloom-producers whose golden flowers sparkle and last up to a week when cut. HOLIDAY CHEER is an ornamental pepper that bushes and tops out at 6 to 9 inches, bringing lively Christmas colors to the summer garden. QUEEN SOPHIA, a dwarf French marigold, has a uniform 10- to 12-inch growth and 2-inch blossoms in a dark bronzy-red color maturing to reddish gold. ORANGE PRINCE is a new frost-hardy pansy with large 2½-inch flowers the shade of ripe apricots. And NICKI-RED is a reincarnation of the nostalgic nicotiana—better known as flowering tobacco—which brings the old-fashioned favorite back in 18- to 24-inch multi-spiked splendor.

An unusual new hop vine, CASCADE, from Mellingers, doubles as an ornamental and brewing-ingredient supplier. A fast-growing perennial sometimes reaching 30 feet in a season, makes a good climbing screen plant for the summer, and has aromatic clusters of papery, pale-yellow hops.

Roses, the world's most popular flower, have a trio of All-America Rose Selection winners available from most mail-order nurseries: SUNDOWNER, a very fragrant, gleaming-orange grandiflora; PARADISE, a distinctively attractive lavender and pink hybrid tea; and FRIENDSHIP, a very hardy, sweetly fragrant pink tea rose.

More flower newcomers of interest to O.G. backyarders include the JOHN WARREN clematis, a soft-gray and carmine 6- to 8-inch bloom from Arthur H. Steffen, Inc. A trouble-free vine plant, the clematis is enjoying new popularity, and several seedsmen have a number of fine new varieties.

A cross between the gladiolus and the fragrant glad has produced the FRAGRANT GLAD-ANTHERA, a delightful full-sized glad-type flower with the pleasant scent of the acidanthera. It's from Henry Field Seed & Nursery, as is HARDY ORCHID, a new cyclamen-pink and purple type that is "half-hardy" and will grow in the open where frost doesn't go more than a few inches deep.

A brilliant-scarlet improved geranium, RED CHAMPION, is from Jos. Harris, along with STARTREK, a gracefully mixed-color blend of grandiflora petunias, and two new profusely blooming French double marigolds, CENTURY GOLD and CENTURY YELLOW.

Park Seed's new "Jolly Geranium" series is a colorful group that's been bred for bushy, base-branching plant growth and 5-inch blossoms flowering right up to frost. Included are JOLLY RED GIANT, JOLLY RED WINK and JOLLY APPLEBLOSSOM PINK.

Burpee ornamentals for '79 feature FANCY PLUMES celosia, a graceful mixture of tall plumes in many colors; HAPPY DAYS, more double French marigolds in rich shades; and SPARKLING BUBBLES, a perennial Iceland poppy that shoots up about 16 inches and blooms in yellow, rose, orange, scarlet and pastel hues the first season from seed.

Stokes Seeds has a fine new group of coleus, along with several other flower introductions. The Fiji coleus series brings 3 new colors, FIJI RED, FIJI SCARLET and FIJI VELVET. SABER ROSE coleus has serrated, swordlike leaves. MINI-GREENSLEEVES and SEVEN DWARFS are compact newcomers developed for close-spaced pot-planting or hanging-basket use. Stokes also has 5 new cyclamen strains, including salmon-red GYPSY that grows attractive flowering houseplants from seed.

Thompson & Morgan has FRECKLE FACE, an unusual new hybrid of the monkey flower (Mimulus) popular in Europe, and good for bedding, tubs and window boxes. Gurney's has SUPER COLOSSAL, a family of new gladiolus bred to grow 6 feet tall, and BLACK PUSSYWILLOW, a striking variation on an old ornamental.

That's just a glimpse of the varieties waiting for the new season. With the promise of so many exciting introductions, plus reliable old favorites, 1979 was truly the year for optimism—a green-thumbs-up year in the garden!

M. C. GOLDMAN

A WINTER'S WORTH OF PEAS FOR TWO HOURS OF WORK

One simple technique gives several major advantages for both peas and gardener.

I'VE SPENT LESS than two hours, total time, working in my pea patch this year, and my pea crop is the best ever. I planted the peas and set up stakes and trellis. No weeding. No watering. I didn't have to. The living mulch of clover in which the peas were planted did it for me.

The rest has been all harvest—and what a harvest! The new SUGAR SNAP peas are known to grow tall (seed catalogs predict six-foot vines), but right now some of my vines are eight feet tall and still growing, and the upper two or three feet of vine are dripping with peas. I could spend this entire article raving about the succulence and sweetness of the SUGAR SNAP—the wonderful, new, eat-all pea that reaches perfection when the peas are large—but that's another story. Here we're going to examine how an inspiration turned into an idea, and how the idea became a method that paid off in unanticipated ways.

The inspiration came from Masanobu Fukuoka's book, *The One-Straw Revolution*, which Rodale Press published in 1978. In that book, Fukuoka describes how he grows rice in fields of clover, and how the clover keeps his work to a minimum. Most of the work we do in the garden or field, he maintains, is unnecessary. We do it only because we think we have to.

So along about midseason of 1978, wanting the clover to form the thickest stand possible, I sowed a whole pound of WHITE DUTCH clover seed in a 25-by-50-foot patch of my garden. Some radish, turnip, beet and carrot seed was mixed in, just to see how the root crops would fare. The idea at this point was to establish a clover bed for planting experiments in the 1979 season. The clover grew fast and overwhelmed the beets and carrots, but the radishes and turnips kept pace and turned out fat roots for our larder. When the clover got a foot high, I cut it back to four inches with a scythe, leaving the cut clover and vegetable tops to decay back into the soil. Before winter arrived, I'd cut the clover three times.

As fall advanced into winter, the clover browned and died back. I realized that, especially on sloping land, the clover roots would hold the soil tightly during winter rains and prevent erosion. It also made it possible to walk in the garden during mud time.

Shane Cox, 6, checks peas just beginning to flower as his sister, Chandra, 4, looks over a clover blossom. Notice the thick mat of living mulch made by the clover.

Then January and February locked everything tightly in ice, and I stayed by the wood stove with my seed catalogs. Reading the entries about SUGAR SNAPS, I got the idea to try peas in the clover come spring. Both peas and clover are legumes, I reasoned, and the established clover roots were well inoculated with the nitrogen-fixing bacteria that inhabit legume root nodules. The presence of such an abundance of beneficial bacteria from the clover should help the peas' nodulation. Also, the previous season's clover would insure that the soil carries enough nitrogen over the winter for the peas to make their best growth.

There was the possibility that the clover, being so thick and strong, would choke out the peas, or use up the potassium, phosphorus and other elements that root nodules cannot manufacture. Still, peas in clover seemed worth the gamble, so I ordered a pound of SUGAR SNAPS for planting in the clover patch.

Winter soon broke, and by the end of March, new clover leaves were unfolding out of the ruins of last season's foliage. I'd originally decided to plant the peas directly in the clover, but now my concern that the clover would choke out the peas got the better of me. I went to the patch with my spade and opened up four single-spade-width rows down the length of the area. As each spade of soil was lifted, I pulled the clover roots out by hand and let the soil drop back in the rows. This whole process took about an hour. On April 1, I planted double rows of peas in each of the four cleared lanes.

The peas came up along with the clover. By the time the peas reached four inches high, the clover had almost covered over the lanes, and in several places the peas had disappeared under the clover. I wondered then whether any of this was going to work.

But peas are climbers and, by the middle of April, they had tendrilled their way above the clover and were in the clear. I set out stakes and stapled pea trellis to them. That took another half hour. From then on, I did nothing but watch it all grow. Any weeds that sprouted were smothered by the thick blanket of clover.

By the time the peas were two to three feet high, the clover had completely filled in the rows I had cleared, and the peas were growing in a thick bed of potential competition. But they didn't seem to mind—in fact, they were huge, healthy-looking plants. A check of the pea roots found them full of big, pink colonies of beneficial bacteria.

Time passed and the pea plants were soon climbing off the top of the five-foot-high trellis I'd given them, flowering as they went. That's when I noticed that the clover was beginning to flower, too.

The clover blossoms brought in all the local bees, and when they were done investigating the clover, they buzzed the airborne pea flowers. Bumblebees, especially, seemed to enjoy the pea blossoms, and there were always dozens of them working the peas, sticking their long tongues deep into the white flowers. This, I thought, meant that when pods developed, they'd be full of peas, not half-empty as in some previous years.

As if to provide more data for the experiment, the weather turned dry at the beginning of June, and by the time pods were filling out, there hadn't been a drop of rain in two weeks. Uncovered soil in other parts of the garden was dry down to three inches. Some tender young seedlings needed watering. I checked the peas every day, waiting for them to wilt in the hot June sun as I had seen peas do during dry spells in past years.

They didn't wilt. The grass had stopped growing, my dirt lane was dusty, my young morning glories were hanging their heads in thirst, but the peas were tall and lush. Then it occurred to me that the clover might be acting as a living mulch, keeping the soil moist under its leaves. It also occurred to me that the clover might be taking soil water from the peas, and could make the water problem more critical. There was only one way to find out, so I got down on hands and knees and pushed the clover apart. The clover was thicker than I thought, and there was a good four-inch mat of leaves and stems before my fingers found the soil—soft, cool and moist.

Not only did the mat of clover keep the soil from drying out, it kept the pea roots cool and shaded—just what peas like during hot June days.

As an added bonus, the turnips that I had allowed to winter over came back up here and there and made beautiful, umbelliferous fountains of green between the pea rows. They set seed, and these seeds will make next spring's turnip crop, free of charge.

The SUGAR SNAPS produced and produced some more. The pods *were* completely filled out. Our freezer is brimming with them, and our main meal every night for a whole week has been taken in the pea patch. We've given lots of peas away, too.

I count this experiment as a resounding success.

JEFF COX

WHAT YOUR TOMATOES CAN TELL YOU ABOUT SOIL DEFICIENCIES

Check your tomatoes against the drawings in this article to see if nutrients are lacking.

TOMATO PLANTS react to various soil-nutrient deficiencies in distinctly different ways. The drawings give an example of a normal tomato contrasted with hunger signs for 12 nutrients.

Diseases, such as viruses, can produce symptoms similar to several of these nutrient disorders. Therefore, if you spot such symptoms on your tomatoes, it may indicate deficiency or disease.

For your next planting of tomatoes, use disease-resistant varieties and make sure you are planting in rich compost made with kitchen garbage. If, for instance, your soil is deficient in boron, kitchen garbage—coming from many foods grown in many places beside your garden—will probably contain enough of the missing nutrients to correct the problem. Manure is also rich in trace elements. Try for a good variety of many different materials, and dig tomato holes to hold a cubic foot of the compost. Trace element deficiencies should clear up in a year if you are adding a ton of manure per 1,000 square feet, plus using lots of mulch in addition to compost right in the plants' root zones.

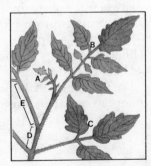

Normal

A normal tomato leaf has good green color and a slightly curved stem. A is the growing point. B shows the young leaves. C shows the old leaves. D is an internode and E is a petiole.

Nitrogen

Leaves show a generalized chlorosis (yellowing). Overall growth is impaired and older leaves drop off. The stems are yellow and rigid.

Potassium

Leaf margins die and leaves are mottled. They curl down, showing a slightly convex upper leaf surface.

Phosphorus

The leaves, especially at the midrib, veins and petioles, darken and show a dull purple tint.

Calcium
   Growing point leaves turn brown at the edges and die back. Young leaves show a purplish-brown tint, while older leaves remain green.

Manganese
   Yellowing occurs in the tissue between the leaf veins, and the leaves appear very mottled. The mottling shows up first on the young leaves.

Magnesium
   Yellowing occurs between the veins. A characteristic green band is apparent on the margins of chlorotic leaves. Young leaves curl up, turn brittle and die.

Iron

Yellowing occurs between the veins on young leaves, especially at the base of the leaflets.

Boron

Light, medium and dark splotches of purple, brown and yellow appear on the leaves. Young leaves have dead tissue. Growing points die back. The stems become stiff and straight. If a teaspoon of borax washed into the soil at the base of the plants immediately solves the problem, it's sure to be a boron deficiency.

Molybdenum

Older leaves show chlorosis or blotches of yellow. Veins remain pale green. Leaf margins die and may roll, giving a convex upper surface. The yellowed areas become puffy.

Zinc

   Abnormally small leaves and internodes. The stems become rough, crack and split (inset), and stem hairs disappear.

Sulfur

   Leaves turn light green, rather than yellow. Growth is poor and stems are spindly.

Copper

   Leaves and stems are spindly and grow poorly and become chlorotic. The leaves curl upwards, showing a definite concavity of the upper surface.

JEAN ENGLISH and DONALD MAYNARD

HOW TO GROW THE "GINSENG OF MUSHROOMS"

The shiitake mushroom has all the health advantages of ginseng—and more!

GINSENG IS a high-priced wild plant that has a remarkable flavor and is thought by the Chinese to have a unique ability to heal the ills and weaknesses of old age. The Japanese know about ginseng and its virtues, but they prefer to seek rejuvenation while eating a mushroom whose flavor beats the taste of ginseng by many miles.

Shiitake is the Japanese name for a type of mushroom that grows in the shape of a flattened umbrella on wood. The taste is unlike that of any mushroom you've ever eaten. One company selling the plant—admittedly with an eye to business—describes shiitake as tasting like "an exotic blend of filet mignon and lobster with the subtle unmistakable hint of mushrooms and to our palates a taste of garlic."

Words like that are enough to make your mouth water on their own, but there must be some truth to them. Dried shiitake shipped here from Japan have been selling for $15 a pound, and locally produced fungi (with moisture) are being sold to fancy restaurants for $2.50 a pound. The market for shiitake is small now, but booming in its own way. Over 500 pounds of shiitake mushrooms can be made to grow on one cord of wood, and word of their great taste and supposed health values is bound to travel fast.

There are two ways to grow shiitake. Under controlled conditions indoors, the mushrooms can be harvested in as little as three to four months. Outdoors, it normally takes up to two years for a harvest, but requires much less work.

A good example of an outside shiitake grower is Stuart Carr, a Maryland farmer who has been experimenting with the mushroom for three years. Working with Byong Yoo, Ph. D., the two have been testing shiitake production on oak wood with good results.

Small holes are drilled into oak logs, and wood chips inoculated with shiitake from Japan are pushed into the holes. The logs

Oak can be felled, implanted with the spores, and left undisturbed until it's time to harvest.

then can be either stacked or left in the woodlot. It takes about two years for the mycelium to impregnate the log and begin fruiting.

In 1974, Dr. Yoo inoculated one cord of oak wood at Carr's farm. The wood was left lying in the woods with no additional care. In 1976, about 110 pounds of mushrooms were harvested and in 1977, another 140 pounds were harvested. "We should have one more year of 140 to 150 pounds, and two years at from 80 to 100 pounds before the logs deteriorate," Dr. Yoo explained. At the lower estimate, that comes to at least 550 pounds of mushrooms from one cord of wood.

"Specialty restaurants in Washington, D.C., are buying all we can produce at $2.50 per pound," Yoo noted. What does farmer Carr think of the potential for growing shiitake in the woodlot? "We've already cut 20 cords of oak and will be inoculating them this fall," he said.

The beauty of growing shiitake outside is that after felling the trees and inoculating the logs, there is no additional labor, except for the mushroom harvest during the spring and early fall. The mushrooms will not survive on living wood, so there is no danger of harming a woodlot. In Japan, logs are stacked and watered and often covered during severe weather to increase yields. But left on their own, they will still produce quite a profitable yield.

Dr. Yoo sells a booklet and kit to inoculate about one cord of wood. The kit includes a drill bit and 500 wood chips. The complete kit costs $21.50, while the booklet ordered alone is $2.50 from Dr. Yoo Farm, P.O. Box 290, College Park, Maryland 20740.

A more involved, and perhaps more profitable, way of growing shiitake has been developed in California. In 1973, Dr. Fred Howard and an associate, R. M. Hoffman, formed the Mushroom Research Institute with the goal of domesticating the shiitake mushroom. After four years, they have developed a process of growing them indoors under controlled conditions that yields a harvest in less than four months.

Instead of natural logs, Howard uses a special growing medium made of oak sawdust and rice hulls. The medium is first sterilized and then inoculated with a special strain of shiitake that Howard cultures himself. Inoculation takes place in a sterile chamber made from a recycled fish tank equipped with ultraviolet light. His process insures that each mushroom is identical, without the possibility of strain variation.

Wood chips impregnated with shiitake spores are pushed into holes drilled in logs.

Handmade growing medium is stored in cans for indoor growing.

Next, the inoculated container is sealed with plastic, which allows air exchange but not contamination. Each can is then labeled, dated and stacked on shelves in ordinary, but slightly subdued, room light.

After three months, what appears to be a log is actually composed of thin strands of shiitake mycelia. The log is placed in a plastic box, watered, sprayed frequently with water mist, and kept at 70 degrees F. Mature bud formation takes several weeks—then, within a matter of days, the shiitake pops out. He isn't sure how long each log will produce, but his educated guess is two years.

The Japanese have been growing shiitake indoors for many years, with results as good as Howard's. The method takes careful climate control and specialized strains that currently are not readily available. Several companies in the United States are woking on kits for indoor production of shiitake, and they should be marketed soon. One kit available is from Thompson & Morgan, Inc., the British seed firm, which has a U.S. address at P.O. Box 100, Farmingdale, New Jersey 07727. Their indoor shiitake kit (for "Black Forest Mushrooms") produces for up to eight months.

Is it true that shiitake has special powers to restore sick people to good health? Your doctor probably would never write a prescription for shiitake, but that may be because he hasn't yet read of studies done in both Japan and the United States which show that spores of shiitake help in cases of influenza and other virus illnesses. One Japanese doctor, Takashi Kaneda, has also shown that shiitake contains eritadenin, a substance which he says has the power to lower the cholesterol content of the blood.

With the growing interest in natural medicines, especially those you can grow yourself, there's bound to be more research into plants like shiitake which have a long heritage of therapeutic use by people like the Japanese. And the fact that shiitake tastes so great won't hurt its cause either.

SHARON MacLATCHIE

COMPANION PLANTING INCREASES YOUR GARDEN'S PRODUCTION!

New results show the value of an age-old method.

COMPANION PLANTING can make a big difference in the amount of food a garden produces. Suppose, for instance, that we have three 4-by-10-foot beds. We plant 12 cabbages alone in one. In the second, we plant 12 wax bean bushes. In the third, we plant 12 cabbages and 12 bean plants together. Which bed will give us the most cabbage? The most beans? The most overall production?

According to the results of this very test at the Organic Gardening Research Center, the third bed scored highest in *all three* categories!

Simply mixing two crops together in one bed—that's interplanting. But when they have a mutually beneficial effect on each other, that's companion planting. The effect may be caused by root exudates that stimulate growth of one or both companions, or to some protective factor in one which suppresses soil diseases harmful to the other, or even to a beneficial shade thrown by one on the other. Science doesn't have firm answers for all cases yet. It may be enough to say—as garden lore has stated through the centuries—that certain plants like each other.

These likes and dislikes are charted in the list accompanying this article. It's meant to be used as a guide, not a rulebook. If you're planning a companionate garden this year, yet find a few places where "unfriendly" plants touch, just consider them experiments and compare their growth and yield to plants surrounded by their buddies. Herbs and flowers are included, too. Besides having benefits for plants grown near them, they disrupt insects' abilities to find their favorite vegetables.

Keep in mind that companion plants are best interplanted, rather than put into contiguous groups. For instance, you can choose from beans, beets, celery, chard, cucumbers, lettuce, onions, potatoes and spinach to plant among your broccoli. Pole beans, however, if staked, might take sun away from the broccoli. Unstaked, they could choke out the broccoli. Unearthing potatoes around the broccoli might disturb its roots. Cukes could climb all over them. Common sense regarding the size and habits of possible companions means you'd probably choose low-growing crops like beets, lettuce, onions and spinach to fill the spaces between broccoli plants. If the companions were put into groups that bordered the broccoli, the companion effect would be lessened.

Take succession plantings into account, too. The lettuce and spinach can mature and be out of the ground before the broccoli has finished production. As soon as they come out, bush beans go in. By the time the bush beans are reaching full size, the broccoli comes out and perhaps late potatoes go in. Thus the bed is kept in successively planted companions throughout the growing season.

Most of the information we have on companion planting is folk wisdom. It was folk wisdom that led American Indians to interplant corn, beans and squash, and the same kind of distilled observation from generations of European ancestors that gave us the companions (just listed) for broccoli. There is some hard scientific information—such as many studies proving that marigolds will clean up soil infested with nematodes even better than most chemical nematocides—but not much. That's why, in 1975, the Organic Gardening Research Center started looking at plant associations.

We started with the familiar bean-corn interplant, supposing that soybeans might fix enough nitrogen through their bacterial root nodules to give a boost to nitrogen-hungry corn. We also planted lettuce with kidney beans, carrots with limas, kohlrabi with cowpeas, and beets and tomatoes with soybeans.

That year we found little nitrogen contribution from the beans in any of the combinations, although there is some nitrogen advantage in the buildup of legume crop residues in the soil over several seasons. Soybeans are good nitrogen fixers, although that nitrogen doesn't get to the interplanted vegetables. Cowpeas are pretty good, and peas and limas are fair at fixing nitrogen. Green and dry beans don't fix much of the nutrient.

We found that the beans are tough competitors and really crowded the vegetables. Bean yields were almost the same as monocropped plots, but the yields of intercropped vegetables were reduced 30 percent. The big exception to this was lettuce among the kidney beans. This trial was done in the hot part of the summer, and the lettuce thrived under the beans' shade. Still, we got a full bean crop and 70 percent of a normal vegetable crop from the space where we would normally have gotten one or the other.

The corn and bean trial was another success that year. We achieved a full corn crop, plus 35 percent of a full stand of soybeans

By mixing low-growing and tall crops, you make maximum use of all the sun's energy that falls on your garden—resulting in higher yields.

in a single field space. Even though the beans didn't feed nitrogen to the corn, neither did they compete for it, preferring to manufacture their own. The corn is tall and airy, the bean low and bushy, able to use the light that falls through the corn canopy. The corn fills its ears in midsummer and is cut, leaving the mature bean plants in full sun to flower and set seed.

In 1976, we tried again. This time we carefully chose low, bushy vegetables to go with tall plants, and we gave our interplants more room. This reduced shading and choking greatly. It was in this season that we found cabbage and wax beans gave better yields interplanted than they did monocropped. Also, staked tomatoes grew as well with soybeans around them as they did alone, but with the bonus of a bean crop 66 percent of normal. Bush beans gave 100 percent of the monocrop yield when grown with carrots, while the carrots turned in a 50-percent yield.

In 1977, we tried three pairings—green beans with peppers, cabbage with soybeans, and potatoes with limas. In the pepper-bean mix, the beans produced a whopping 54 percent more than monocropped beans. The peppers came in with a crop 64 percent of the monocropped plot.

Interplanted cabbage yielded 23 percent better than mono-cropped, while the bean yields were unaffected—which is to say, there was a good bean crop and an even better cabbage crop.

Potatoes planted with limas didn't pan out very well. Both stands looked good, but the limas produced so few pods that they weren't worth harvesting. Furthermore, it was difficult digging the mature tubers without damaging the limas.

This past summer we began looking at pairing compatible vegetable shapes, such as fat with skinny, tall with short, deep root feeders with shallow root feeders. No results yet. And after that, we'll be studying various companions again to round out our knowledge of this phenomenon.

There are two practical guidelines that we've pulled from our results so far. First, if you plan to mix beans with their companion vegetables, favor the companions. Give them enough space to avoid being crowded out by the beans. The beans are tough and can take crowding. Second, dense interplanting requires good, rich soil improved the organic way. If you are taking out twice the vegetables from the same space in your harvest basket, you have to have twice the nutrition in the soil. That means early manuring, sidedressings in the summer, and a handy barrel of manure tea.

A final generalization is that vegetables whose flavors and textures harmonize on the table probably also make good companions in the garden—a la succotash. We found that yields of several vegetables soared way past those of monocropped plots when set out among friends. You can take advantage of this, too. Here, in a list prepared by Alfred Beltran of Bismarck, North Dakota, and expanded with further information from our experiments and files, is all you need to know to plant a companion garden.

Companions, Allies and Enemies in Your Garden

In the following listing, companions refer to those vegetables that, when planted together, are mutually beneficial. Allies are the herbs and flowers that provide protection or improve the growth of certain vegetables. Enemies are other vegetables, herbs and flowers that can cause detrimental effects when planted near certain vegetables.

This listing explains in detail the exact effects of the allies and enemies, and names the companions.

ASPARAGUS: Companions: Basil, parsley, tomato

Allies: Pot marigold deters beetles.

BEAN: Companions: Beet (to bush beans only), cabbage family, carrot, celery, chard, corn, cucumber, eggplant, pea, potatoes, radish, strawberry

Allies: Marigold deters Mexican bean beetles and nematodes.

Nasturtium and rosemary deter bean beetles.

Summer savory deters bean beetles, improves growth and flavor.

Enemies: Garlic, onion and shallot stunt the growth of beans.

BEET: Companions: Bush beans, cabbage family, lettuce, onion

Allies: Garlic improves growth and flavor.

Enemies: Pole beans and beets stunt each other's growth.

CABBAGE FAMILY: (Broccoli, Brussels sprouts, cabbage, cauliflower, Chinese cabbage, kale and kohlrabi)

Companions: Beet, celery, chard, cucumber, lettuce, onion, potato, spinach

Allies: Chamomile and garlic improve growth and flavor.

Catnip, hyssop, rosemary and sage deter cabbage moth.

Dill improves growth and health.

Mint deters cabbage moth and ants, improves health and flavor.

Nasturtium deters bugs, beetles, aphids.

Southernwood deters cabbage moth, improves growth and flavor.

Tansy deters cabbageworm and cutworm.

Thyme deters cabbageworm.

Enemies: Kohlrabi and tomato stunt each other's growth.

CARROT: Companions: Bean, lettuce, onion, pea, pepper, radish, tomato

Allies: Chives improve growth and flavor.

Rosemary and sage deter carrot fly.

Enemies: Dill retards growth.

CELERY: Companions: Bean, cabbage family and tomato
    Allies: Chives and garlic deter aphids.
    Nasturtium deters bugs and aphids.
CHARD: Companions: Bean, cabbage family and onion
CORN: Companions: Bean, cucumber, melon, parsley, pea, potato, pumpkin, squash
    Allies: Odorless marigold and white geranium deter Japanese beetles.
    Pigweed raises nutrients from the subsoil to where the corn can reach them.
    Enemies: Tomatoes and corn are attacked by the same worm.
CUCUMBER: Companions: Bean, cabbage family, corn, pea, radish, tomato
    Allies: Marigold deters beetles.
    Nasturtium deters aphids, beetles and bugs, improves growth and flavor.
    Oregano deters pests in general.
    Tansy deters ants, beetles, bugs, flying insects.
    Enemies: Sage is generally injurious to cucumber.
EGGPLANT: Companions: Bean, pepper
    Allies: Marigold deters nematodes.
LETTUCE: Companions: Beet, cabbage family, carrot, onion, radish, strawberry
    Allies: Chives and garlic deter aphids.
MELON: Companions: Corn, pumpkin, radish, squash
    Allies: Marigold deters beetles.
    Nasturtium deters bugs and beetles.
    Oregano provides general pest protection.
ONION: Companions: Beet, cabbage family, carrot, chard, lettuce, pepper, strawberry, tomato
    Allies: Chamomile and summer savory improve growth and flavor.
    Pigweed raises nutrients from subsoil and makes them available to the onions.
    Sow thistle improves growth and health.
    Enemies: Onions stunt bean, pea.
PARSLEY: Companions: Asparagus, corn, tomato
PEA: Companions: Bean, carrot, corn, cucumber, radish, turnip
    Allies: Chives deter aphids.
    Mint improves health and flavor.
    Enemies: Garlic and onion stunt the growth of peas.
PEPPER: Companions: Carrot, eggplant, onion and tomato

POTATO: Companions: Beans, cabbage family, corn, eggplant, pea

Allies: Horseradish, planted at the corners of the potato patch, provides general protection.

Marigold deters beetles.

Enemies: Tomatoes and potatoes are attacked by the same blight.

PUMPKIN: Companions: Corn, melon, squash

Allies: Marigold deters beetles.

Nasturtium deters bugs and beetles.

Oregano provides general pest protection.

RADISH: Companions: Bean, carrot, cucumber, lettuce, melon, pea

Allies: Chervil and nasturtium improve growth and flavor.

Enemies: Hyssop

SPINACH: Companions: Cabbage family, strawberry

SQUASH: Companions: Corn, melon, pumpkin

Allies: Borage deters worms, improves growth and flavor.

Marigold deters beetles.

Nasturtium deters squash bugs and beetles.

Oregano provides general pest protection.

STRAWBERRY: Companions: Bean, lettuce, onion, spinach, thyme

Allies: Borage strengthens resistance to insects and disease.

Thyme, as a border, deters worms.

Enemies: Cabbage

TOMATO: Companions: Asparagus, carrot, celery, cucumber, onion, parsley, pepper

Allies: Basil repels flies and mosquitoes, improves growth and flavor.

Bee balm, chives and mint improve health and flavor.

Borage deters tomato worm, improves growth and flavor.

Dill, until mature, improves growth and health. Once mature, it stunts tomato growth.

Marigold deters nematodes.

Pot marigold deters tomato worm and general garden pests.

Enemies: Corn and tomato are attacked by the same worm.

Mature dill retards tomato growth.

Kohlrabi stunts tomato growth.

Potatoes and tomatoes are attacked by the same blight.

TURNIP: Companions: Pea

JEFF COX

FAST COMPOST WITHOUT MANURE!

If compost shortages are a perennial problem, here's a sure-fire way to multiply your present output.

VICTOR DALPADADO MAKES fast composting sound easy, and he's right to paint a simple picture of it. Hardly anyone knows how to make a compost pile that matures in two weeks, yet it's about the most useful technique imaginable. Most people think fast composting requires special methods, special materials and a special knack. Not so.

Consider what some regard as essential to composting—layering brush on the bottom, alternating layers of the different materials, shredding everything, mixing in some earth, using a bacterial starter, adding chicken manure, counteracting acidity with lime or wood ashes. But not one of these things is essential to the process that Dalpadado has outlined so clearly.

On his way to teach compost making in Ecuador, Victor Dalpadado stopped to tell us about the system which he developed in his homeland of Sri Lanka. When he first began experimenting, he was working as an agricultural extension agent and he wanted to develop a composting business for people in the capital city who had no daily work, but scavenged for their sustenance. Over a three-year span, working with these people and the process, he boiled composting down to its basics.

There are five things to concentrate on when making fast-acting compost, according to Dalpadado.

1. *Vary the materials* to make a balanced food supply for the microorganisms.

2. *Mix all materials thoroughly* instead of making layers.

3. *Make many scratches* and cuts in the stems and leaves to provide entry for microorganisms.

4. *Turn frequently* for aeration.

5. *Maintain ample moisture*.

Before explaining exactly how to do all those things, I should tell a litttle about how Dalpadado developed his process. He started his study of composting with the classic Indore method (named after the state in India where Sir Albert Howard formulated this basic composting process). Most gardeners use some variation of the Indore method when they make compost. Piles are made by alternating different materials and perhaps are capped with earth. If the piles are turned once or twice, the compost may be fully digested in six months. With no turning it takes a year.

For the business that Dalpadado foresaw, six months or even three months for decomposition was too long. There were several other restricting conditions that he had to resolve as well. Poverty ruled out any equipment but the simplest hand tools. There were no livestock manures or stable sweepings such as Sir Albert had, but nearby was the city dump with a regular supply of garbage and some wastepaper. Aquatic weeds grew abundantly in nearby waterways. Dalpadado saw that key ingredients were on hand for the taking. Moreover, he knew compost would be a salable item. Gardeners need it because organic matter doesn't last long in Sri Lanka's hot, sandy soil.

'Gems from Garbage'

So for three years Dalpadado and the compost makers critically examined every step in the process, and learned what things were important and what weren't. Today the people make compost on a very regular schedule, using only machetes for chopping coarse materials and 10-pound, hoe-type mattocks for turning the piles. Groups of three people each, package and sell about 15 tons of compost a month under the name *Kasala Menik*, "Gems from Garbage." Each day a team builds a new pile six-by-eight and three feet high, about a ton of material. They turn the older piles that need turning, and bag and sell the finished piles of odorless compost, now reduced to about a half ton. They have made themselves a profitable and steady business.

To make a fast compost pile, Dalpadado says it is most important to learn how to blend all the varying materials that can be collected, to provide a balanced food supply for the decay organisms. No single material is right by itself. But when the materials in a heap together present a certain proportion of nutrients, the bacteria and fungi work rapidly. Nitrogen, a building block of protein for bacterial reproduction, and carbohydrate for an energy source, are all that matter. The major reason that compost piles don't maintain high heat and rapid decay is a shortage of nitrogen-rich materials. Manures are very high in nitrogen, which is why some people regard manure as the essential ingredient in a successful compost. But Dalpadado's system is proof that manure certainly isn't necessary.

Ideally the ratio of carbon (carbon content is the usual way that soil scientists gauge carbohydrate) to nitrogen in a well-made compost pile should be 30 to one. In practice, however, the precise amount of either carbon or nitrogen is extremely hard to determine, and knowing the number is not important as long as the pile is working well. Use the carbon-to-nitrogen-ratio concept as a general guideline, in conjunction with the average values in the accompanying chart. Then let experience teach you. For a rule of thumb, Dalpadado says that the proportions should be roughly two-thirds of high carbohydrate sources, which tend to be drier, somewhat tough and woody (dry leaves, stems, straw, paper) to one-third of green succulent materials high in nitrogen. Any soft, fresh green matter like young weeds or grass clippings is high in nitrogen.

It is always better to put on a little too much of the nitrogen-rich material. Without enough, the pile won't heat properly. And the only negative effect of having a little too much nitrogen is that the excess will be lost as a gas when the pile is turned.

Always Enough Nitrogen

Sri Lanka's people rely mainly on vegetable matter in garbage and the leaves of water hyacinth for nitrogen in the compost. To insure that the piles reach high heat rapidly and hold it, the composters also add their urine, which they collect each day for that purpose. And when the high-nitrogen vegetable matter is in very short supply compared to the amount of stalks and paper which they must use, half of the new pile is made with half of an active, partially decomposed pile. Thus there is always a way to get enough nitrogen into the newly started pile.

A word about urine. Urine from people who aren't sick is essentially sterile, and so it can be used safely. It is not at all like fecal wastes in this respect. And urine is very valuable used this way because it is high in nitrogen, containing about half of our total nitrogen wastes, as well as being rich in phosphorus and potassium. Furthermore, the very high heat engendered in this method of composting is a failsafe. If any pathogens happened to be present, the heat would destroy them, as several studies have shown. Nonetheless, when plenty of green matter is available, the vegetation contains all the nitrogen needed for fast compost.

After gathering together materials in the right proportions to feed microorganisms, the second step toward fast composting is to mix the material uniformly. Stacking them in layers as in the traditional method is an excellent way to keep track of the balance that you are trying to create. But the layers themselves get in the way of a true nutrient mix. Dalpadado has found it best to thoroughly mix all the materials and then make the final stack.

The third requirement for fast composting is to break and bruise the skin of the plant materials as much as possible. Dalpadado points out that a primary function of the skin of all plants and animals is to resist the attacks of bacteria and fungi. Everyplace the skin on stems and leaves is opened—even if only a bruise or scratch—provides an entry point for decay organisms. This is the most important thing that a shredder does to speed composting. But the skin of plant materials can be broken very effectively by hand methods. In Dalpadado's system, all large materials are first cut into six-inch lengths with a machete. Then the piles are formed with the large, sharp mattocks, and later turned with them too. In the process, the materials are beaten, raked and scraped, rather than lifted and turned as you might do with a pitchfork. The larger pieces of stem and stalk which are slowest to decay are completely crushed and scarred this way.

This way of turning has the added advantage of exposing all particles to the air at each turning. No large clumps can survive intact as they can when turned with a fork. Complete and frequent aeration is Dalpadado's fourth major element in rapid composting. Active decomposition is a process akin to burning, and air is used up rapidly especially at the start. Dalpadado recommends that the first turning be made on the second day after the heap is built. Turn it again on the fourth day, then again on the seventh day, and on the tenth. After the last turning, the temperature of the pile should begin its drop from the 140- to 160-degree F range down to 110 degrees F, at which point it is finished and ready to use.

The fifth thing a compost pile needs is ample moisture. Under the surface, the material should glisten with moisture without being soggy. Many times fresh green materials can provide most of the moisture the pile needs. A lot of water goes off in steam at turning, however. In dry weather Dalpadado recommends watering the pile at the start until water begins to seep out of the bottom. It is good to protect the pile from drenching rains with black plastic, since excess water can drive oxygen out of the pile, leach out nutrients, and drastically lower the temperature.

Trying the Method with Leaves

I tried this system and was delighted and amazed to watch it work just as Victor Dalpadado had described. I started with an enormous amount of leaves stored over winter in plastic bags. Leaves, I felt, would be a good test of the fast composting because they are so tough and mat so tightly. In previous composting attempts, leaves had always taken many months to decompose, seeming to slow the action more than helping it. The only other materials I used were grass clippings, which are easy to find bagged on any trash day, and some vegetable wastes from the kitchen. The only tools I used were a spade, a pitchfork and a long-stemmed soil thermometer.

Grass clippings, of course, are shredded very nicely to start with. I figured they would be all the nitrogen the pile needed. From prior experience I anticipated that grass could putrefy into gummy lumps if left in thick pieces. So I carefully estimated proportions of the materials and homogenized them. The pile heated up within hours.

It was fascinating to see the process going like clockwork. By the third turning at the end of a week, everything had become a uniform dark brown. I mixed in five gallons of fresh garbage three times, and each time the material was completely digested by the next turning. Even eggshells seemed to disappear. The pile stayed about 140 degrees F the entire time, and once reached 160 degrees F. At each turning the temperature would drop to 100 degrees, but regain full temperature within eight hours.

Turning the pile was a real workout. I used the pitchfork like a mattock, cutting a vertical section through the pile with the tines. This ripped through the leaves and broke up remaining mats. The first two turnings required 45 minutes. (The pile was six-by-three by three feet high.) Later turnings took half that. Chopping instead of lifting was a tiring but satisfying experience.

For one thing, it is obvious from the start that the microbes liked what was happening. The thermometer gave a clear reading on that. Another indication was the healthy fungal activity. Mycelial strands covered everything in the outer eight to 12 inches of the heap. To make sure that fungi worked on everything, I chopped through the outer layer of the top and sides where the gray-white fungus showed and moved this to form the center of the new pile. The old central material in turn became the outer layer, covered with fungi at the next turning. In the second week, all this breakdown had made chopping and turning much easier.

By the 18th day, the temperature had gradually declined to 110 degrees F. The compost was nearly odorless. In fact the pile had never smelled foul. The only strong smell was a tinge of ammonia at turning, a sign that I had probably put on a little too many grass clippings. The compost was black and lumpy. Pieces of leaves were recognizable only on close inspection.

The best sign of a properly made compost pile is the temperature. When it rises fast and maintains heat over two weeks, the nutrient mix is right. Another good sign is when the temperature rises back to full heat within 24 hours after a turning. A good compost pile should be nearly odorless throughout the process.

Another sign that the pile is finished is the temperature dropping to 110 degrees F no matter how often you turn it. The material should be dark and rich. If the material has not been shredded, things like paper and leaves will still be recognizable, but they are finished composting and ready to apply to the soil. They won't rob the soil of nitrogen. They can be made to break down further by more turning, but the extra work would be counterproductive.

Fast Compost is the Answer

Garden soils can in time become rich enough that one or two moderate applications of compost a year are enough to maintain fertility. A slow and easy Indore-type compost heap is all you need then. But when the soil is low in humus, or when the composting area is so small that a few batches per year don't make enough to go around, the fast compost method is the answer. An actively pursued program of two-week composting translates into at least eight batches ripening for use during the growing season.

There are other advantages than speed that should not be overlooked. Fast compost is the highest quality. Adding actively decaying organic matter gives a greater boost to soil microorganisms, insects and earthworms. Their activity feeds the plants. The compost itself is as rich in nutrients as it can be, since it hasn't been leached by the rains that drench long-term heaps time and again. The mechanics of the system are perfectly suited to the gradual accumulation and efficient use of relatively small amounts of wastes which most of us face. All of these things are very important when compost is at a premium in your garden. Victor Dalpadado's good work and generosity have done all of us gardeners a big favor.

JACK RUTTLE

A MICROBIAL FEAST

TO MAKE A BLEND of materials that approaches the ideal 30 to one, you need to determine the carbon-nitrogen ratios of the materials you have. Things that have low values for carbon are the "rich" materials that must be diluted by adding more materials with carbon values above 30. If you have leaves and fresh grass to work with, and if you assume leaves are worth 50 and grass is worth 20, then a pile made with equal weights would have a carbon-to-nitrogen ratio of 35 to one. This is very good, but it can be brought down to 30 by adding a little more grass. If you should smell a lot of ammonia as this pile works, you might figure that those leaves have more nitrogen than 50 to one, perhaps 40 to one. Next time you build the pile, use more leaves and less grass. Forming the pile according to volume, you would probably have to add a greater amount of leaves, since they are fluffy and much lighter than a same-sized pile of grass clippings.

CARBON/NITROGEN RATIOS
of VARIOUS ORGANIC MATERIALS

Food wastes (table scraps)	15-1
Sewage sludge: activated	6-1
digested	16-1
Wood	700-1
Sawdust	500-1
Paper	170-1
Grass clippings	19-1
Leaves	a range of 80-1 to 40-1
Fruit wastes	35-1
Rotted manure	20-1
Sugar cane residues	50-1
Cornstalks	60-1
Straw	80-1
Alfalfa hay	12-1
Humus	10-1
Alfalfa	13-1
Green sweet clover	16-1
Mature sweet clover	23-1
Legume-grass hay	25-1
Oat straw	80-1

SOLAR SALAD GREENS – THE GREAT NEW TASTE for FALL

These little-known Oriental vegetables are so much more productive than lettuce that you should reconsider your customary plans for fall planting.

OUR WORK WITH the solar greenhouse at the Organic Gardening Research Center has changed our ideas about cold season gardening in ways we never dreamed of when we started several years ago.

We found out, for instance, that a humble cold frame, with a few changes, can become a substantial producer of fresh food. By incorporating the best ideas from the greenhouse into several new cold frame designs, we've picked fresh salad greens from the unheated frames right through the winter.

Another discovery—the best salad crop for these structures is not lettuce! We found that the special environment inside the solar structures transforms almost *all* leafy vegetables into good salad plants. Even more important, we've come upon a large and diverse group of little known Chinese vegetables—mostly in the cabbage family—that outproduce traditional cold weather vegetables.

You've never had salads like you get from these plants! They overwhelmed us, frankly, when we realized how well they were growing and how fine they tasted. In the cooler temperatures and less intense light under glass in autumn and winter, the leaves and stems of all vegetables grow thinner, more tender and less fibrous than you would expect. They all take on the texture of lettuce. They are exceptionally sweet, too, perhaps because the plants are making more sugar during the day than they can use up before night chills growth to a stop. The Chinese vegetables thrive under these conditions and grow fast.

We sought out these new plants because the ordinary cold-hardy vegetables that we started with grew so slowly. We surmised that they were poorly suited to the cool damp weather and short days inside our greenhouse. After all, they've been bred for the kind of climate most of America experiences in the frost-free

78

period. Spinach, for example, we thought would be our big solar greenhouse crop. It grew so reluctantly as a winter crop that we practically gave up on it. (Lately we've found a better greenhouse spinach, MONOPPA.) Keeping lettuce free of mildew required more care than we were used to giving it. The large cole crops and the cold-tolerant root crops grew too slowly and yielded too little food to warrant giving them much space in the beds. What grew best for us were kale, chard, endive and parsley, and we got fair salad production from them. But we knew that in other places—parts of Europe and China came to mind immediately—varieties had been

The makings for many fine salads grow all winter in our free-standing solar greenhouse. Now's the time to get ready to grow them.

developed especially to grow outdoors right through the damp, chilly and overcast end of the year. And many of those vegetables have come through for us very well indeed.

We did best getting varieties from China and Japan, thanks largely to the many Oriental gardeners on the West Coast and their seed suppliers. Nearly all of their varieties recommended for the cold season have grown wonderfully in the solar greenhouse and cold frames. All the ones we're recommending here not only grow big enough for the first harvests to begin in 40 to 50 days, but they also rebound from pickings very rapidly with new leaves or side-shoots. They've raised the productivity of the solar structures considerably. And they make exciting salad blends. Typically, a salad bowl will be filled with tender leaves from 15 to 20 varieties of leaf vegetables and salad herbs. You can recognize bits of kale, red chard and lettuce here and there, but the bulk is made up of these still strange and wonderful new plants. Here are the ones that our experience suggests will do best for you.

SIEW CHOY (*Brassica pekinensis* var. *cylindrica*), looks like a tall version of savoy cabbage if allowed to mature. The leaves are very wrinkled with a large celerylike midrib. But as with nearly all of these plants grown for winter salads, we pick the outer leaves continually and let the plant grow. The large midrib as well as the tender leaves are excellent fresh, remaining juicy, mild and tender despite their size. This is a good plant for cold frames, since it won't get much over eight inches tall.

SEPPAKU TAINA (we have been unable to find its scientific name) is a beautiful plant with soft, broad leaves growing at the end of pure white stalks, which are also very sweet. It grows in a tight bunch like celery and so can be planted very close together. It will make some growth even at 45 degrees F, and the leaves keep their good eating quality after hard freezes.

BOK CHOI (*Br. chinensis,* var. *chinensis*) is the familiar Chinese cabbage, but its outer leaves stay tender and uncabbagey in the cold frames. Pick it regularly and don't allow the 10- to 14-inch heads to form. These leaves also are unaffected by temperatures in the mid 20's.

CHOY SUM (*Br. parachinensis, Bailey*), the Flowering White Cabbage, is grown for its sweet flower stalk, a bit like raab broccoli in appearance. It does not form a loose head like the others, but begins to send up the stalk very early. Cut the entire plant and chop leaves, stem and buds for salads or stir-frying.

DAI GAI CHOI (*Br. juncea* var. *rugosa*) forms a very loose and upright head. The leaves are quite curly and grow out of a

These rare Chinese greens—most of them crucifiers—come in all sizes and shapes.

prominent midrib. Pick the outer leaves. The flavor is sweet and peppery.

GAI CHOI (*Br. juncea* var. *foliosa*) also has a mild mustard flavor, but it forms more green leaf and less stem than Dai Gai Choi. It grows very fast. The plant is a small one and should be spaced six inches apart.

KOMATSUNA (*Br. pervidis Bailey*) looks more like young broad-leaved chicory than a cabbage. The small oval leaves are extremely green, tender and mild. It is the slowest growing one we've tried, but it is an excellent choice for the cold frame because it is extremely cold tolerant and compact in habit. Set plants six inches apart.

KYO MIZUNA (*Br. juncea,* var. *multisecta*) is the strangest brassica you've ever seen. It forms a bushy rosette of narrow feathery leaves, like a very wispy endive plant. Its flavor is mild and pleasing; it looks great in salads and grows fast.

SHUNGIKU (*Chrysanthemum coronarium*) is fairly well known as an Oriental potherb, but we found that it is an excellent candidate for the salad bowl. The three-inch shoots are succulent and tangy, and the plant readily produces more when clipped back all winter.

We find that it's best to establish a healthy mix of these plants before the onset of really cold weather and short days. However, it's also important not to let the cold frame air temperature get too hot for them (ideally nothing over 70 degrees F, but that can be tough to achieve and most of these plants tolerate extremes well). After harvesting the outer leaves continually, a long stem develops and productivity slows. Then we remove the plants and replace them with transplants two to four weeks old. Starting seeds in the cold frames can be done in cold weather, but we find that starting them indoors under ideal conditions makes for healthier plants and best use of cold frame space.

These are not vegetables that you will find on the seed racks of the average garden center. You'll have to order them from catalogs. Give yourself plenty of time to get seed, because these are extra special food plants that will add considerably to your late season food supply.

Seed Sources

Seed companies with good selections of cold-hardy Oriental vegetables include:

Herbst Brothers Seedsmen, Inc.
100 North Main St.
Brewster, New York 10509

J. L. Hudson, Seedsman
P.O. Box 1058
Redwood City, California 94064

Tsang and Ma International
P.O. Box 294
Belmont, California 94002

Grace's Gardens
Autumn Lane
Hackettstown, New Jersey 07840

Kitasawa
356 W. Taylor
San Jose, California 95112

R. H. Shumway
Rockford, Illinois 61101

STEVE GANZER, DIANE MATTHEWS, and
EILEEN WEINSTEIGER

GARDEN ALL WINTER WITH SOLAR GROW FRAMES

Proven in use at our Research Center, these new designs make cold-weather gardening possible in every state.

FORGET THE THOUGHT that you need oil or other fossil fuel to heat a greenhouse for growing winter vegetables. Now, with the latest in solar technology, you can build a simple, inexpensive solar structure that will produce the best salad greens all winter long.

The old cold frame is the basis of this new idea, but it's been changed to catch and store every useful ray of the winter sun's heat. And it's small, so almost everyone can build one.

Best of all, these new structures have been tested in use—some for two complete winters. Ten different solar grow frames have been built at the Organic Gardening and Farming Research Center. Over 10,000 different temperature readings have been taken inside them during winters so cold they set new records month after month. Yet these mini solar greenhouses stayed warm enough to produce fine salad greens during February and March.

The idea behind the solar grow frame is simple. Each different type has a well-insulated frame that is sealed tightly to keep air from leaking in. And the glass or plastic covering on the south side is double thickness, with an air space between the layers. There must also be a removable cover or opening so you can reach every part of the growing area easily from the outside. The best solar grow frames also have a heat storage area inside, which serves mainly to keep the frames from getting too warm during sunny winter days.

The first year, our Research Center tested five grow-frame designs.

A-Frame

This unit is a simple, inexpensive design with uninsulated plywood walls, shaped like an A. The south side is glass, the north side and the ends plywood. No thermal mass is added to the frame. Only the soil is used to store heat. The frame is insulated 10 inches below ground level.

83

Stone-Pac

The design incorporates insulation 10 inches below soil level and on all sides, plus 72 cubic feet of concrete slabs added to the north wall for heat storage. The north-facing wall and parts of the sides are bermed with earth to further protect against freezing.

Water-Pac

Identical in all other respects to the stone-pac, this design uses 180 gallons of water in five-gallon cans for heat storage, instead of concrete.

The Pod

Shaped like a large, flat bubble, the pod uses a two-layer fiberglass covering over the growing bed, with only the ends made of wood. The soil is insulated to a depth of 10 inches. Designed by Leandre Poisson, the bubble can be lifted completely off the bed. No additional thermal mass is added—the unit depends solely on the soil for heat storage.

The Can

Also designed by Leandre Poisson, this unit uses insulating beads between the two layers of south-facing fiberglass to reduce heat loss at night. It is insulated on all sides to a depth of 10 inches below ground level. During the day, the insulating beads are stored in a cylinder at the top. A flip shutter allows the beads to flow between the two layers of glazing at night. In the morning, the front is lifted and the beads return to the cylinder by gravity. The shutter is moved to keep the beads in place during the day.

During that first winter we learned that the potential for solar grow frames was much greater than we had originally hoped. Most of the frames operated successfully through the entire winter. Average minimum air temperatures were in the mid 30's, with soil temperatures in the low 40's, despite an extremely cold winter.

We designed five additional frames for testing the next year. Temperatures inside the frames were dropped close to freezing the first year, so we looked for ways to add extra heat without using fuel. Our main approach was to capitalize on the heat produced by the composting process. To do that, we built manure hotbeds below several of the frames. We also experimented with separate composting chambers, as well as with a solar hot-air collector, and with special cold-hardy plants.

We decided to extend the depth of the in-ground insulation to 24 inches, while staying with our original design of an outside layer of fiberglass and an inside layer of polyethylene. We improved weather-sealing techniques, and reduced the size of the openings from full-front to a smaller hatch that enabled easy access, yet was easier to seal, lift and handle, and didn't let so much cold air in.

The five new frames we built were of two basic styles—above-ground and belowground. All 10 frames were wired with special devices to record temperatures in the air and at several soil depths. These are the second-year grow frames.

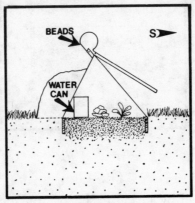

Manure Pit

The frame is built around a two-foot-deep layer of composting horse manure, which furnishes heat. A pit is dug four feet deep and insulated on all sides and the bottom. Two feet of fresh horse manure, plus a foot of soil on top are added, making the growing surface one foot below soil level. The rest of the frame is insulated on all sides, with the nonglass sides bermed to protect them from winter winds.

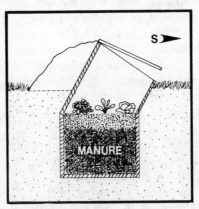

No-Manure Pit

We built this grow frame exactly like the manure pit, but insulated it to a depth of only two feet, including the bottom. A

86

one-foot layer of soil is used in the growing area, with no manure, again placing the growing surface one foot below ground level.

Manure A-Frame

It's insulated on all sides, including the bottom, and placed against the south wall of a building. A hole three feet deep is dug, insulated, and filled with two feet of manure and one foot of soil. The growing surface is at soil level.

Manure Bin

One of two freestanding cold frames we experimented with, the manure bin incorporates a well-insulated, aboveground growing bed with movable bins to hold composting manure below the growing beds. Under the one-foot-deep growing bed, a pair of two-foot-deep bins of manure is positioned. The entire unit is shuttered at night with insulation to hold in heat. The unit is placed against the south wall of a building.

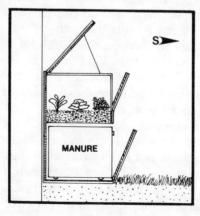

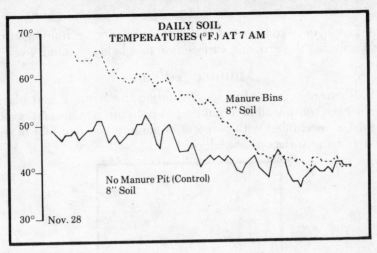

The heating effect of manure across the growing season is shown in this chart. The manure-heated soil started out a good 15 degrees warmer than the standard soil, but by the end of the season, the temperatures were equal.

The Sauna

Another aboveground design, the sauna is quite similar to the manure bin unit, only it uses a hot-air solar collector instead of manure to generate heat. The collector picks up heat during the day, and vents it through a convective loop to a rock bed below the growing bed. At night the rocks give off heat to the growing bed, keeping the soil warm. The entire unit is wrapped in insulation to hold in heat at night.

Our results the second year were outstanding! Some of the frames cruised through the entire winter, never dipping below the 30's, despite consecutive below-zero days outside. We found that even though many of the units had similar thermal performance, plants did better in some units than others.

We learned that the level of insulation for an all-winter growing unit should be no less than R-11 (a rating of resistance to heat flow) on all walls. That is best achieved with two inches of Styrofoam, a material not affected by moisture. Although the no-manure pit was designed to serve as a check for the manure pit, it showed us the importance of enclosing the entire growing bed with insulation, especially the bottom. It performed almost as well as the manured units, despite not having the additional heat supply, and was warmer than any of the other units with no additional heat supply. We also learned that 24 inches of insulation below ground level works much better than the first year's 10 inches.

Earth berming offers little advantage, compared to insulation. It requires additional structural strength, and may not be worth the extra cost. However, it does have a moderating effect on temperatures. Putting the growing bed below soil level offers no thermal improvements, and makes it more difficult to work.

We found that plants will tolerate cold air temperatures if their roots are warm. Warm soil provides extra heat exactly where it is most needed, and releases heat into the environment.

Manure can be a most effective heat source, providing steady heat throughout the growing season. We found that manure with a lot of straw in it worked best for the growing beds, as it composted more gradually, giving off heat over a longer period of time. The manure and sawdust mix that we used in the bins heated up quickly, but also cooled off quickly. We started our manure beds too early in the season, in mid-October. If manure beds are started in December, they should provide heat throughout the worst of the winter season.

In the first year we used night shutters on all frames. The second year none were used, and a comparison showed that the use of an insulating cover over the glass at night can increase the air temperature by as much as six to 10 degrees. All solar grow frames should have some type of insulation over the glass during the night.

The use of thermal mass helped only marginally to heat the grow frames, but seemed to aid the growing vegetables. However, it did moderate some of the peak temperatures on extremely warm or sunny days, protecting the plants from overheating and reducing the need to vent the frames. The thermal mass was above soil level, and thus did not place heat where it was most needed—in the soil. Any heat given off by the mass heats the air at night, which is not as important as heating the soil. However, the thermal mass may have a radiant heating effect on the plants. We are not sure. We do know that the two units with thermal mass produced better plants than units without mass, although they all recorded similar temperature readings.

In addition to our lessons on grow-frame performance, we've picked up a number of pointers on designing and building the units. The two key factors are access and durability. You have to have an easy way to get inside the frames to work on the plants, and the frames have to withstand almost constant exposure to moisture and the forces of winter.

We have found that, above all, you should be able to reach all corners of the frame from one of the openings. It is best to have an inside height of at least 36 inches so you can work comfortably inside the frame.

However, the door openings should be as small and as lightweight as possible. In many cases you will be opening or closing the doors with only one free hand. The opened door should lie securely against the structure so it won't shut in a gust of wind.

Being able to remove the entire glass face, so you can easily work the entire soil bed, is a handy arrangement. On the manure beds, this is most important, as you will have to dig out the old manure each year and refill the bed.

The biggest lesson we learned is that it is a lot harder to build an underground wooden structure than we thought it would be. The combination of constant moisture, decaying manure, frost heaving, fluctuating temperature extremes between the inside and outside of the frames, and general drainage problems played havoc with our frames. Openings constantly came ajar, foundations lifted, water leaked into the growing beds, and so on. Our designs worked, but our construction techniques left a lot to be desired.

We now know that a thin film of condensation covers every surface inside the frames all winter. Weep holes and drainage channels will eliminate most pools of standing water, but you pay a price in increased infiltration. Horizontal surfaces should always be avoided. Wherever we had a horizontal top on a frame, water would collect, forming ice.

Any parts you feel will deteriorate rapidly should be designed to be easily replaced. Use bolts or screws rather than nails. When buying hardware, stainless steel is best, followed by aluminum, brass and galvanized steel. Cadmium-plated or zinc-plated steel hardware will rust in about a year, and most likely will fail within two or three years in an underground situation.

Naturally preserved woods such as cedar, locust and cypress

are the only woods with any reasonable life expectancy in a cold frame. To protect wood surfaces, apply a 1/16-inch coating of either asphalt foundation sealant, Gilsonite paint, or brush on an acrylic coating. The asphalt materials are the most durable for underground use, and the white acrylic coatings are best aboveground. Avoid wood preservatives like pentachlorophenol.

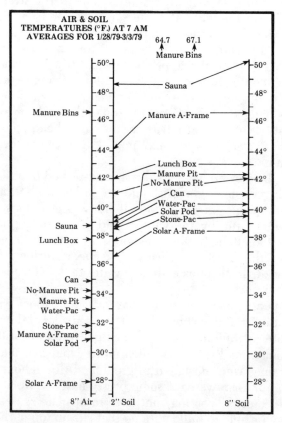

For a period slightly more than one month, soil and air temperatures were monitored simultaneously and charted

Styrofoam insulation must be protected from both the sunlight and errant shovels. If it is on the outside of the frame, ultraviolet rays will gradually deteriorate it. On the inside, unless you are extremely careful, it can be damaged while you're working the soil. We will try sandwiching the foam during winter in hopes of protecting it. The foam will be between two layers of 1/4-inch plywood, with wood-stud framing for support. These sandwich walls will be bolted or screwed together and waterproofed.

More than half of the light reaching plants during the winter is diffuse rather than direct, in most parts of the country. A sloping back, found in several of the frames we used, has no advantage as far as trapping light. For maximum light inside the frame, a vertical rear wall is best. The sloping walls create extra stress on the structure due to the weight of the soil used for berming. White paint is the best color to use inside the frame for bouncing light to the plants. Most grow frames began to overheat when outside temperatures reached the upper 30's, with strong sunshine. Your grow frame should have some provision for venting excess heat.

We may be putting two vents in our new frames, one on the side for incoming air, the other at the top of the back for exhausting air. You only want to vent a bare minimum of heat, since all heat vented is heat lost, and you may need that heat the next day or even that night.

Lastly, be sure to have good drainage. A bed of at least three to four inches of small gravel should be under the bottom insulation, with drainage gravel around all sides. The frames normally stay quite moist during the winter, and you should not have to water them too often. If a leak develops and water comes in from the outside, the frames can easily become waterlogged, setting back plant growth. In areas with high water tables consider putting your entire frame aboveground.

Some people may find that a masonry foundation, with Styrofoam insulation, is the best bet. It will prevent a lot of the problems we encountered building with wood underground, will provide additional mass, and won't be much more expensive than wood.

Our frames were designed to grow food throughout the winter, and on our farm we have some pretty nasty winters. In other areas of the country, you may not have to insulate as deeply or at all. You may be able to build a frame that sits on top of the ground and depends on hay bales for insulation. In short, we were working with the most advanced designs. You'll be surprised at how well a simple grow frame with a little insulation will perform if you plant the right crops—especially the cold-weather Chinese vegetables we described in the previous article. We aren't trying to create summer during the winter inside a grow frame. It's more like trying to turn winter into fall. If you can keep soil temperatures in the 40's, you'll be successful.

We will be building new frames for the Research Center. We will again test such ideas as manure hotbeds, thermal mass, insulat-

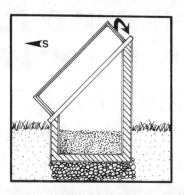

This year, all experiments will be conducted in grow frames like this. It features small doors, a vertical rear wall, both deep and bottom insulation and well-sealed openings. A thermal curtain will be added.

ing night curtains, as well as new crops for grow-frame gardening. We've learned a lot about what goes into a good grow frame, and feel that our new designs will work better than any of the previous models, and that they will last longer. The art of gardening in miniature greenhouses in the ground is just starting.

Ray Wolf

93

NOW BUILD THIS —
THE SUNFLOWER SEED
HULLER AND OIL PRESS

Vegetable oils used to be one of those items you just had to buy. Now here's how to make your own.

IN 2,500 SQUARE FEET, a family of four can grow each year enough sunflower seed to produce three gallons of homemade vegetable oil suitable for salads or cooking and 20 pounds of nutritious, dehulled seed—with enough broken seeds left over to feed a winter's worth of birds.

The problem, heretofore, with sunflower seeds was the difficulty of dehulling them at home, and the lack of a device for expressing oil from the seeds. We decided to change all that. The job was to find out who makes a sunflower seed dehuller or to devise one if none were manufactured. And to either locate a home-scale oilseed press or devise one. No mean task.

Our researches took us from North Dakota—hub of commercial sunflower activity in the nation—to a search of the files in the U.S. Patent Office, with stops in between. We turned up a lot of big machinery, discovered how difficult it is to buy really pure, unrefined vegetable oils, but found no small-scale equipment to dehull sunflowers or press out their oil.

The key to success, however, was on our desk the whole time. In spring, 1977, August Kormier had submitted a free-lance article describing how he used a Corona grain mill to dehull his sunflower seeds, and his vacuum cleaner exhaust hose to blow the hulls off the kernels. A second separation floated off the remaining hulls, leaving a clean product. We'd tried it, but because some kernels were cracked and the process involved drying, we hadn't been satisfied. Now we felt the best approach was to begin again with what we learned from Mr. Kormier and refine it.

Staff Editor Diana Branch and Home Workplace Editor Jim Eldon worked with a number of hand- and electric-powered grain mills. While the Corona did a passable job, they got the best results with the C. S. Bell #60 hand mill and the Marathon Uni Mill, which is motor-driven. "I couldn't believe my eyes the first time I tried the Marathon," Diana says. "I opened the stones to one-eighth inch, and out came a bin full of whole kernels and hulls split right at the seams. What a thrill that was!"

She found that by starting at the widest setting and gradually narrowing the opening, almost every seed was dehulled. The stones crack the hulls open, then rub them to encourage the seed away from the fibrous lining. The Bell hand mill worked almost as well. "As long as the stones open at least as wide as the widest unhulled seed, any mill will work," she says.

Because the seed slips through the mill on its flat side, grading is an important step to take before dehulling. We made three sizing boxes. The first is ¼-inch hardware cloth. The second is two layers of ¼-inch cloth, moved slightly apart to narrow the opening in one direction, and the third is two layers of screen adjusted to make a still-smaller opening. Since the smallest unhulled seeds are about the size of the largest hulled kernels, the grading step prevents these undersized seeds from passing through unhulled. Processed together at a closer setting, the smallest seeds hulled out.

Jim Eldon's workshop is littered with strange-looking pieces of apparatus. They represent initial attempts to build a workable winnowing box, using Kormier's vacuum exhaust idea for a source of air. Jim, Fred Matlack and Diana finally made a box with a Plexiglas front, through which they could observe what was happening. They cut a hole in the back of the box with a sliding cover to regulate the air pressure, and fiddled with various arrangements of baffles. The result was a stream of hulls exiting through one hole while the kernels fell to the bottom of the box. Now they were ready to try a five-pound sample of unhulled sunflower seeds to see how much they could recover.

The five pounds were graded and dehulled, then winnowed. We got about one hull for every 10 kernels in the final, winnowed product. These are easily picked out. They usually contain kernels still held behind the fibrous strings of the hull. Their weight prevents them from blowing out with the empty hulls. We found that bug-eaten seeds do blow away with the chaff, which was a bonus for cleanliness of the final product. Toss the hulls to the birds, who will find broken seeds among them.

Starting with 80 ounces of unhulled seed, we ended up with 41¼ ounces of edible whole seeds, 1.8 ounces of damaged seeds suitable for animal feed, and 36.6 ounces of hulls. It took us about an hour. Not bad.

Sunflower seeds store perfectly in the hulls, but they deteriorate more rapidly when shelled out. The grain mill dehuller and winnowing box give the gardener a way to have the freshest possible seeds for eating at all times of the year. With the construction of one more piece of equipment—the oil press—he can have absolutely fresh, unrefined, polyunsaturated sunflower oil for salads, mayonnaise and cooking.

Most light, refined vegetable oils have been extracted using hexane, a form of naphtha. The oil is then heated to boil off the hexane. Lye is dumped into it. It's washed with steam, then heated to remove odors and taste before being laced with preservatives and stabilizers. It may feel oily in the mouth, but you might as well taste air. Not so with fresh-made sunflower oil—it's deliciously yet subtly nutty in flavor, adding unsurpassed flavor to salads.

There's good reason to believe that sunflower oil may become the #1 vegetable oil in the United States in a few years. It's already #1 in health-conscious Europe. Corn oil has already caught on here for health reasons, and sunflower oil is so much better. Sunflower oil's 70 percent polyunsaturate is just under safflower, with corn oil bringing up the rear with 55 percent. And sunflowers yield 40 percent oil, soybeans only 20 percent.

Our oil press is relatively simple, but it must be welded together. Check the construction directions for details. The press consists of a welded tubular frame which accepts a three-ton hydraulic jack. You may already have one. If not, it can be purchased at most auto and hardware stores for about $16. A metal cannister with holes drilled in its sides and one end welded shut holds the mashed sunflower seeds. A piston is inserted in the cannister and then inverted and slipped over a pedestal on the frame. The jack is set in place, and the pressure gradually increased over half an hour. The oil drips from the sides of the cannister into a tray—the bottom of a plastic jug slipped over the pedestal works fine—which empties the oil into a cup. You can filter the oil with a coffee filter to remove pieces of seed and other fine particles that would burn if the oil were used for cooking. If it's for salads or mayonnaise, there's no need to filter it.

We first tried using "confectionary" sunflower seeds for oil. These are the regular eating kernels we're used to seeing. They give less than half as much oil as the oilseed types of sunflower. Although you can use confectionary types such as MAMMOTH RUSSIAN for oil, don't expect to get more than an ounce and a half from a pound of seed. Oilseed produces three or more ounces of oil from a pound of seed and is well worth planting along with confectionary-type seeds. Oilseed has another big advantage—to prepare it, you can put the whole, unhulled seed into a blender and whiz it until it forms a fine meal, while confectionary seeds must be dehulled first. The entire sequence of grading, dehulling and winnowing is avoided with oilseed.

Oil types produce about a tenth of a pound of seed per head in commercial production. Gardeners, with their better soil and care, invariably do better than that. Our conservative estimate is that 1,280 plants will be enough for three gallons of oil. Spaced one foot apart in rows two feet apart, 1,280 oilseed plants will take a space 40-by-56 feet, or 80-by-28 if you want a more rectangular patch to face south.

We worked in pound batches, since the cannister just holds one pound of mash. After blending, we heated it to 170 degrees F by placing it in a 300-degree F oven and stirring it every five minutes for 20 minutes. Heating gets the oil flowing and doubles the yield of oil. In case you're wondering, "cold-pressed" oils sold commercially are also heated, and some are subjected to the entire chemical process. The term has no firm meaning within the industry, according to the literature we've surveyed.

Heating does not change the structure of fats. It will not turn polyunsaturated fats into saturated fats. In fact, Dr. Donald R. Germann in his book, *The Anti-Cancer Diet*, says that ". . . an unsaturated fat must be heated to high temperatures—above 425 degrees F or 200 degrees C—at least 8 or 10 times before any shift toward saturation occurs. . . ." Dean C. Fletcher, Ph.D., of the American Medical Association Department of Foods and Nutrition in Chicago, says, "It's true that either high temperature or repeated heating does change the nature of some of the unsaturated oil molecules. (But) the flavor of the oil changes as these chemical changes occur, spoiling its taste. This effect is probably more profound than any of the physiological changes the altered oil might produce within the body."

From 500 gm. of heated mash, we pressed 89 gm. of oil, 89 percent of the entire amount available and twice as much as we could press from unheated oil! The decision is up to you whether or not to heat the mash, but that extra 50 percent seems like an awful lot, especially when the whole technique is so labor intensive. The oil should be stored in the refrigerator, and it's probably best to use it within a month, since it has no preservatives. Mayonnaise made with such fresh oils should be kept refrigerated and used within two weeks. The leftover cake, still containing 50 percent of its oil, is a nutritious addition to your dishes, and makes excellent feed for animals or winter birds. Store the pressed cake in the freezer.

We're talking then about a sunflower patch with two kinds of plants—confectionary such as MAMMOTH RUSSIAN and oilseed

97

such as PEREDOVIK. The oilseed plants should be grown 12 inches apart in rows two feet apart. Four average confectionary heads yield about a pound of unhulled seed. You'll need about 35 pounds of unhulled seed, or 140 plants worth, to yield 20 pounds of hulled kernels, about what a family of four will use in a year. That many plants can be grown in an area 26-by-10 feet. That's 260 square feet. Put that together with the 2,240 square feet for the oilseed sunflowers, and you need a patch about 2,500 square feet—25 100-foot rows—to keep yourself supplied year-round with super nutrition and unsurpassable taste.

Winnowing Machine for Sunflower Seeds

The winnowing machine operates on the age-old principle of blowing the chaff away from the heavy grain with a controlled current of air.

The unit uses a household or shop type vacuum cleaner for its air supply. A vacuum cleaner was used as a power source because it can supply a large volume of air over an extended period of time, and most homes and farms have a vacuum cleaner.

A cloth bag has been attached to the chaff chute to catch the chaff as it is separated from the seed. The bag allows the hulls to be collected and greatly reduces the amount of waste material normally blown into the air by conventional cleaning systems.

The unit has been constructed in such a way that the cloth bag and cleaner box can be placed inside the seed box, making a compact package for storage.

Tools Required:
1. Table Saw
2. Drill Press
3. Band Saw
4. Saber Saw

Procedure: (cleaner box)
1. Cut out the two sides of the cleaner box from ¼-inch plywood.
2. Cut out the six interior pieces of the cleaner box from 3/4 x 3½-inch select pine.
3. Assemble the cleaner box elements with glue and nails.
4. Cut four ¼-inch square strips of pine four inches long.
5. Glue the strips around the end of the chaff chute.
6. Sand all surfaces and edges.
7. Finish with clean lacquer finish.

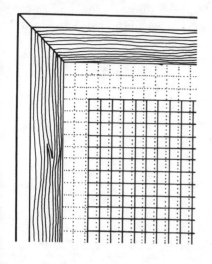

A *hardware cloth grader sizes the kernals for better hulling. Two layers of cloth, spaced slightly apart, narrow the hole for a second grading. The more grading, the better the hulling.*

Procedure: (seed box)

1. Cut two pieces of pine ¾ x 5½ x 15 inches for the sides.
2. Cut two pieces of pine ¾ x 5½ x 8½ inches for the top and bottom.
3. Plow a ¼ x ¼ groove for the front and back panels in all four pieces.
4. Rip the top board to 5 inches so that the front panel can slide into the grooves in the side boards.
5. Rabbet both ends of each 15-inch side piece to accept the top and bottom boards.
6. Drill a hole in the left side board 2½ inches from the top. The size of the hole is determined by the vacuum cleaner hose fitting.
7. Cut a 3¼ x 4-inch hole in the top ½ inch from the right end. This hole will accept the cleaner box.
8. Cut two pieces of pine for the baffle.
9. Drill two 1-inch holes in the bottom of the baffle box.
10. Cut a piece of ¼ x 8½ x 14-inch plywood for the back panel.
11. Cut a 3-inch hole, centered 1⅞ inches from the top and left sides of the plywood back.
12. Assemble the sides, baffles, top, bottom, and back panel with glue and nails.

13. Cut a 8⁷/₁₆ x 15¾-inch piece of ¼-inch Plexiglas for the front.
14. Cut a one-inch radius on the top corners of the front and sand the edges.
15. Drill a one-inch thumb hole centered ⅞ inch from the top edge.
16. Cut a 3½-inch disk of ¼-inch plywood for the vent cover.
17. Drill a ³/₁₆-hole ⅜ inch from the edge of the disk.
18. Mount the disk over the vent with a #10 x 1-inch screw.
19. Sand all surfaces and edges of the box.
20. Finish with clear lacquer finish.

Materials

ITEM	PCS.	DESCRIPTION	COST INCLUDING SCRAP
Cleaner Box			
Sides	2	7¾ x 7½ x ¼″ plywood	$ .22
Baffles	6	¾ x 3½ x 24″ for all members	1.20
Chute Cleats	4	¼ x ¼ x 4″ pine	.05
Nails	22	1″ x 18 ga. headed	.08
Glue	—	White vinyl glue	.10
Finish	—	Clear lacquer finish	.30
		Subtotal	$1.95
Seed Box			
Sides	2	¾ x 5½ x 15″ select pine	$2.70
Top and Bottom	2	¾ x 5½ x 8½″ select pine	1.20
Baffle	1	¾ x 3½ x 4½″ select pine	.20
Baffle	1	¾ x 4¼ x 4½″ select pine	.30
Back	1	¼ x 8½ x 14″ plywood	.30
Control Valve	1	¼ x 3½″ dia. plywood	.05
Front	1	¼ x 8⁷/₁₆ x 15¾″ Plexiglas	1.10
Screw	1	#10 x 1″ flat head screw	.05
Nails	18	4d finish	.10
Glue	—	White vinyl glue	.10
Finish	—	Clear lacquer finish	.50
		Subtotal	$6.60
Bag	1	17 x 31″ cloth laundry bag	1.40
		Total	$9.95

100

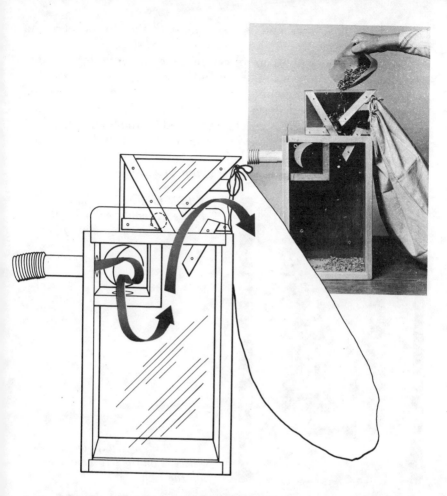

A simple winnowing box using forced air from a vacuum cleaner exhaust and some baffles propelled hulls into the collection bag as whole kernels dropped into the box.

Sunflower Seed Oil Press

The press was designed so that homesteaders can produce sunflower oil from their own seeds. The oil can be pressed as is or heated to 170 degrees F, which doubles oil yield.

Both methods require the seed to be ground to a fine powder. If you are pressing the oil seed variety, a meat grinder or electric blender will do an excellent job of grinding the seed. The confectionary type of seed will require the seed to be hulled and winnowed before it is ground. A food mill with the stones set at the coarse setting can be used to accomplish this step.

The ground kernels are placed in the cylinder with the piston closing the bottom portion of the cylinder.

The cylinder is mounted in the press frame and a three-ton hydraulic jack is used to supply the pressure.

Because of the great pressures created by the hydraulic jack it is important that the frame be properly constructed and firmly mounted to the work surface before the pressing operation begins. The following instructions can be given to a welder.

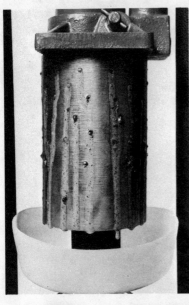

A little heat and the oil pours out of the pistonlike cylinder, then to be strained with a paint filter.

Two kinds of sunflower seeds— oilseeds on the left, confectionary on the right.

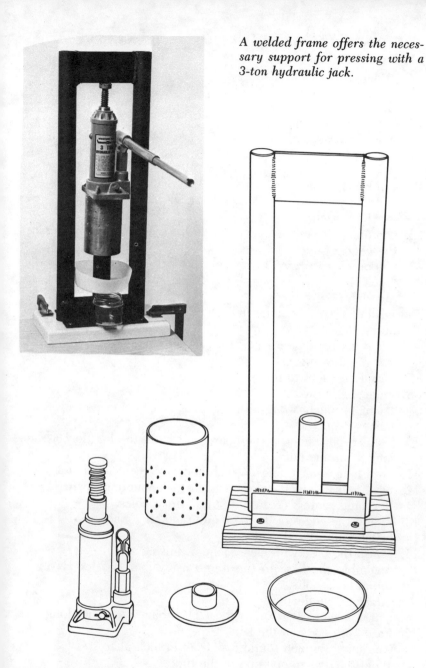

A welded frame offers the necessary support for pressing with a 3-ton hydraulic jack.

Secure welds on all parts are needed because of the high pressure exerted to squeeze the oil from the seeds.

Tools Required:
1. Power Hacksaw
2. Metal Band Saw
3. Metal Lathe
4. Drill Press
5. Belt or Disk Grinder
6. Arc Welder
7. Hand Clamps

Procedure: (Frame)
1. Cut two pieces of 1¾ O.D. x 1⅜ I.D. x 24½-inch-long tubing for the uprights.
2. Cut one piece of 1¾ O.D. x 1⅜ I.D. x 6½-inch-long tubing for the center tube.
3. Cut one ¾ x 2¾ x 5½-inch steel bar for the top cross member.
4. Cut two pieces of 1¾ x 1¾ x 8-inch angle iron for the base members.
5. Drill two $9/32$-inch holes in each base member ½ inch from the outer edges.
6. Weld the base members, tubes and cross member together as per the drawing.
7. Grind all edges to remove any burrs.
8. Paint the frame.
9. If a mounting board is desired, cut a piece of pine 1¼ x 6½ x 12 inches long.
10. Center the frame on the board and mark the location of the four mounting holes.
11. Drill four ⅞-inch holes ¼-inch deep to accept the T-nuts.
12. Drill four $5/16$-inch holes through the mounting board using the same centers created by the ⅞-inch holes.
13. Round the edges of the base and sand all surfaces.
14. Install four ¼-20 T-Nuts.
15. Finish the base with clear lacquer finish.
16. Assemble the base to the frame using four ¼-20 x 1¼-inch round head bolts.

Procedure: (Cylinder)
1. Cut a piece of 3½ O.D. x 3¼ I.D. tubing 5⅝ inches long.
2. Face both ends on the lathe.
3. Cut out a 3½-inch round disk from ¼-inch plate steel.
4. Weld the disk to one end of the tube.
5. Drill a series of $3/32$-inch holes around the side of the tube on ½-inch centers.
6. Remove all burrs on the inside and outside of the tube.

Procedure: (Piston)

1. Cut out a 3⅜-inch disk of ¼-inch plate steel.
2. Cut a 1⅜ O.D. x 1⅛ I.D. piece of tubing 1⅛ inches long.
3. Face both ends of the tube.
4. Weld the tube in the center of the 3⅜-inch disk. All welds should be made on the inside of the tube.
5. Mount the piston in the lathe and turn the disk to fit the inside diameter of the cylinder. This will be about 3¹⁵/₆₄ inches in diameter.
6. Remove any sharp edges.

Procedure: (Collector Ring)

1. Cut the bottom out of a one-gallon plastic bottle. The cut line should be approximately 1½ inches from the bottom of the bottle.
2. Make a ⅛ x 1-inch slot at one edge of the bottom outside ring. This will allow the oil to pour into a receiving cup.
3. Cut a 1¾-inch hole in the center of the bottom so that the unit will fit over the center tube in the frame.

Materials

ITEM	PCS.	DESCRIPTION	COST INCLUDING SCRAP
Frame			
Frame tubes	2	1¾ O.D. x 1⅜ I.D. x 24½" long H.R.S.	$ 4.50
Center tube	1	1¾ O.D. x 1⅜ I.D. x 6½" long H.R.S.	.55
Top cross member	1	¾ x 2¾ x 5½" flat bar H.R.S.	.73
Base members	2	1¾ x 1¾ x 8" angle iron H.R.S.	1.10
Wood base	1	1¼ x 6½ x 12" #2 white pine	.75
Mounting bolts	4	¼-20 x 1¼ R.H. bolts	.32
T-nuts	4	¼-20 T-nuts	.40
Finishing material	—	Black enamel for frame	.50

ITEM	PCS.	DESCRIPTION	COST INCLUDING SCRAP
Finishing material ... —		Clear lacquer finish for wood base	.10
Welding rods 3		⅛ dia. welding rods	.30
		Subtotal	$ 9.25
Cylinder			
Top 1		¼ x 3½ dia. C.R.S. disk	.40
Cylinder 1		3½ O.D. x 3¼ I.D. C.R.S. tube	1.10
Welding rod 1		⅛ dia. welding rod	.10
		Subtotal	$ 1.60
Piston			
Piston top 1		¼ x 3⅜ D.A. C.R.S. disk	.40
Piston tube 1		1¼ O.D. x 1 I.D. x 1″ long H.R.S.	.15
Welding rod 1		⅛ dia. welding rod	.10
		Subtotal	$ .65
Collector Ring			
Oil collector ring 1		Bottom from a one-gallon plastic bottle	N/C
		Grand Total	$11.50

JEFF COX

NEW GRAPES ON OLD VINES

Now we can graft grapes the way we graft apples.

A RECENT development by scientists at the Experiment Station in Geneva, New York, makes it possible to graft grapes to maintain production on the old vine while the grafted part grows to maturity.

If you have a grape variety that is not up to expectations for some reason or another, you can now graft on another variety that

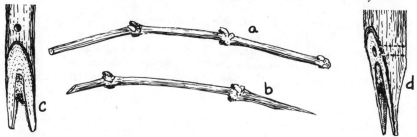

Start with a pencil-sized cane with three buds (a) for the scion. Make one diagonal cut 1½ inches above the top bud (at left in b). Make a straight cut 3 inches below the bottom bud. Drill a thin nail hole 1⅛ inches from the bottom of the scion.

Slice the scion into a wedge starting ⅛ inch below the nail hole for the outside surface (c) and ⅛ inch above the nail hole for the inside surface (d). The inside surface will face the grapevine trunk when grafted. The outside face should be an inch long, the inside about 1¼ inches.

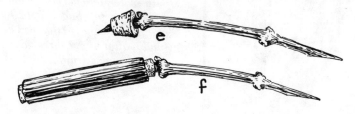

A cork with a hole through the center is pushed over the top, down to the thickening above the top bud (e). Be careful not to damage the bud. A tube, such as a piece of old garden hose, is fitted over the cork so the fit is watertight (f).

Select a straight portion of the trunk and peel off loose bark. Wrap a piece of ¾-inch grafting tape around the trunk (g). This is very important. The bark is ringed with a single cut all around the trunk 1 inch above the tape (h). Two cuts the approximate width of the scion are made from the ringing cut to the edge of the tape (i) to form the flap under which the scion will go.

The wedge end of the scion is inserted under the flap with the inside face to the trunk and pushed down as far as it will go (j). The nail is gently driven in (k), and a grafting rubber is used to hold the graft securely (l).

The tape is removed and draped between scion and trunk. Tree-wound compound is used over the tape and the graft (m). The tube is filled with water and a top cork with no center hole is used to close the tube (n). Keep the tube filled with water by checking it once a week. The top bud should burst and form a cane (o) that can eventually, after about three years, be used as a new trunk.

may grow better in your region, even the new seedless grapes. In about three years, the new vine will start to bear. By the fourth year you should be getting a good crop. The old vine can be cut off just above the graft after the third or fourth year, leaving an entirely new vine.

To begin, you must select cuttings from the vines you wish to propagate. If you have none of your own or can't get them locally, a wide variety is available from the New York State Fruit Testing Association at Geneva, New York. Cuttings should be taken when the vines are dormant, before any sign of bud burst. The cuttings are taken from the past season's growth and should be as thick as a pencil. As you take your cutting, be sure that all the top buds are facing in the same direction. Bundle them, identify the tops with a marker and label the variety. Place them in a plastic bread bag long enough to enable you to tie the end. Add a handful of moist (not wet) sphagnum moss, seal the end of the bag and store them in the refrigerator (temperature approximately 40 degrees F). They should remain there until you are ready to graft. An occasional inspection of the cuttings should be made to be sure that the moss has not dried out.

The grafting is done about the first week in June when the bark on the old vine loosens easily.

An excellent booklet, very well illustrated, which goes into great detail on this subject is available for just $1. It's entitled "Converting Mature Vineyards to Other Varieties," by Keith H. Kimball, Special Report #22. Order from the New York State College of Agriculture and Life Sciences, Cornell University, Ithaca, New York 14850.

PETE LYPKA

WHITEFLIES
FINALLY CONTROLLED!

At last, a simple, yet completely organic way to get rid of one of the toughest cold-frame and greenhouse pests.

TWO USDA SCIENTISTS have finally found a safe and sensible way to control whiteflies. Their control technique doesn't call for any chemicals, companion plants or the like. They simply paint small boards yellow, cover them with a sticky substance, and hang them in the greenhouse. The flies are attracted to the yellow color, and become stuck to the boards.

Although it sounds simple, the results are nothing short of fantastic. I visited Dr. Ralph Webb in his laboratory at Beltsville, Maryland, and he demonstrated the new technique. We went to a greenhouse where the experimental whitefly population is reared. There, holding a piece of white paper about 18 inches from a tomato plant that was literally covered with whiteflies, he shook the plant. The flies immediately took wing and hovered around the top of the plant for a few seconds, before settling back on it. Then, substituting a yellow board for the pad paper, he shook the plant again. I was amazed to see about 70 percent of the flies go directly to the board. As Dr. Webb had promised me, "They are attracted to the board like iron filings to a magnet."

Working with Dr. Floyd Smith, Webb has been experimenting with the whitefly control method since 1970. "Originally we needed a nonchemical way to control whiteflies while we experimented with other insects in the greenhouse," he recalled. Having read of earlier work on color attractance of insects by Dr. James Kring, he began to experiment with different colors and methods of use. Finally he decided on using an orange-yellow, as it had a far higher attractance rate than any other color.

The use of the sticky boards in other experiments was so successful that Dr. Smith convinced Webb they should do a controlled experiment to test just how effective the control method was. The results surprised even the two researchers.

In one experiment, the treated boards were placed between infested tomato plants. The whitefly population was reduced by about 25 percent each day. In a second experiment on chrysanthemum plants, 12 treated boards completely eliminated a whitefly infestation within 24 hours.

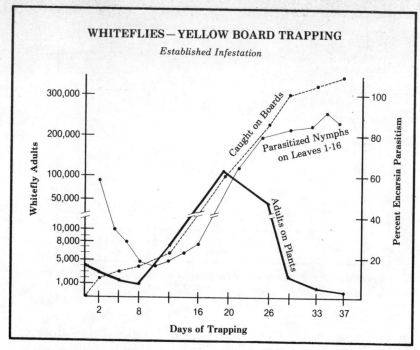

WHITEFLIES — YELLOW BOARD TRAPPING

Established Infestation

Using both sticky boards to control flying adults and a wasp to parasitize the larvae, Dr. Webb reports that whitefly control has been "well beyond what commercial growers aim for."

In the most exciting experiment, the researchers combined the boards with a parasitic wasp (*Encarsia formosa*) and had what Dr. Webb calls virtually absolute control. The boards controlled the flying adults, and the parasites controlled the nymphs.

Because of their mobility, once in a greenhouse, whiteflies quickly spread throughout an entire building. That, combined with a life cycle of about one month, gives the whitefly a reputation as one of the toughest of all insects to control. The stationary boards are very effective at attracting a high percentage of the flies, since they travel around so much during a short period of time.

There are two ways to use this control method, Dr. Webb explained. A treated board can be hand-held and individual plants shaken to get rid of an intense population outbreak quickly. Or, you can hang the treated boards in the greenhouse, and they will control an existing population.

Webb has found that the boards work best when they measure about one foot square. He uses Rust-Oleum 659 yellow paint, but

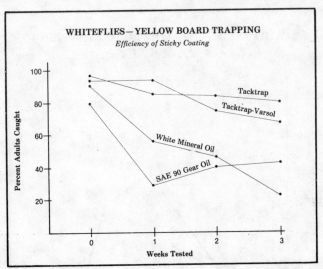

WHITEFLIES — YELLOW BOARD TRAPPING
Efficiency of Sticky Coating

Tacktrap

Tacktrap-Varsol

White Mineral Oil

SAE 90 Gear Oil

Percent Adults Caught

Weeks Tested

Commercial sticking agents make traps that work nearly a year. For home use, heavy motor oil or mineral oil will do the job fine.

other similar shades would work as well. For the sticky substance, he has found that a product called Tacktrap gives the longest period of control, working for up to a year or more. However, they have also had good results with other commercial trapping agents. They also have used SAE 90 motor oil and heavy mineral oil. For short-term use, the mineral oil has an effectiveness of from two to three weeks, and the motor oil about two weeks.

The only problem with the control method that Smith and Webb can find is that the sticky boards can be a nuisance hanging around the greenhouse. To solve this problem, the two researchers tested different cages to keep the boards in. After experimenting, they found that a green wire, with about a two-inch-square mesh opening worked best. Smaller mesh sizes reduced the effectiveness of the trap, but the two-inch opening proved as effective as the uncaged boards, yet kept people and plants from getting stuck.

To use the traps, Dr. Webb recommends a minimum of four treated boards for about every 150 square feet of greenhouse space. The boards should be hung right in the middle of the plant canopy, as whiteflies do not fly upward, but travel laterally. Once the boards are treated, they need no further care until they are either completely covered with trapped insects, or, if using mineral oil or motor oil, they lose their stickiness. Then all you have to do is clean off the boards, retreat them, and forget about whitefly problems.

RAY WOLF

MAKE THESE SAFE PESTICIDES IN YOUR KITCHEN BLENDER

The more we learn about the backyard blender sprays, the more we like them.

WE ARE SLOWLY awakening to the notion that insect pests can be handily controlled by substances available in our own yards.

Six years ago, Eleanore Bubb of Sun City, Arizona, inspired by a report in ORGANIC GARDENING, wrote to tell us that she had solved an intractable problem with western grape skeletonizer by whizzing some of them in a blender with water, then spraying the strained liquid back on the grapevines. Two years later, Mike Sipe, a Florida pest control specialist, used the idea to rid a 100-acre peanut patch of its pests. The bug juice method was born.

So far, readers, other publications, and scientists have reported that the bug juice method works successfully on over 20 insects, including cabbage looper, grape skeletonizer, stink bug, armyworm, velvet bean caterpillar, granular cutworm, ants, slugs, fungus gnats, sawfly worm, aphids, wireworm and several species of caterpillar. In this article, we'll look at new results of this technique and its sister, the plant juice method, also first suggested by Eleanore Bubb. The latter uses locally occurring plant extracts to curb pests.

We tried the bug juice method on Colorado potato beetles at the Organic Gardening and Farming Research Center last year, but the results were inconclusive. We've redesigned the test and will be trying it again this year, along with the plant juice method.

There's plenty to report from readers and even from the scientific literature. These consummately simple methods are beginning to win a following.

Our Research Center staff can expect success with its potato beetle trials, if the experience of Jim Cressman in Frankfort, Kentucky, is an indication. He says that, "Last year I tried the bug juice method on the striped (Colorado) potato beetle. I'm happy to tell you that they all disappeared within a week and we had no more trouble with bugs in our potatoes the rest of the season."

"Everything contains the seed of its own destruction," reasoned the woman who first tried the bug juice method.

The method works down in the Tropics, too, where the insects are big and voracious. Melinda Troutner, a researcher at the Center for Tropical Agronomy in Turrialba, Costa Rica, grew an experimental garden with 10-foot rows of beans. She tried the method on local insects that attack the beans. "Immediately following the application, it was obvious the insect populations in the treated plots were extremely low (one or two insects per 12 feet of row), while the untreated plots had normal populations (four or five insects per plant). Daily observations since this time have been less dramatic," she says, indicating the need for a weekly reapplication until pest levels decrease for keeps.

Not all the answers are in on bug juice. Several readers reported negative results, and one scientifically controlled study done in South Africa showed that cutworm extract actually attracted, rather than repelled, cutworms. We'd be grateful if you'd report your results to O.G. Reader Service, Bug Juice Test.

On the plant juice side, we have this encouraging report from Patty Aleshevich of Anchorage, Alaska:

"I recently noticed that one of my houseplants was infected with mites. I flashed on your plant juice article and decided to give it a try. I gathered a handful of leaves from a poplar tree in our yard and blended them with water. You suggested the mixture steep for a day, but I couldn't stand the sight of those mites, so I sprayed immediately.

"After several hours, I checked the plant—no mites! The next day, although I couldn't spot any mites, I gave the plant another dose. Three weeks have now passed without a single mite, and my plant and I are *very* pleased!"

What's happening here? Paul Feeny and a group of researchers at Cornell suggest the answer in the June 16, 1978, issue of *Science*. They report that allylglucosinolate, found in the leaves of most cabbage-family plants, is acutely toxic to the caterpillar of the black swallowtail butterfly. By contrast, they found that an insect that specializes in eating cabbage could ingest all the allylglucosinolate they could give him without harm.

"Certain compounds in plants may serve as qualitative barriers to plant-eating insects," Feeny says, meaning that if we can get those compounds in solution and onto our crops, the bugs will go looking for something else to eat. In the case Feeny cites, the plant extract was actually insecticidal. We expect that most successful plant juice extracts will repel, rather than kill, the pest. This is a plus in the organic garden, where the idea is to establish a natural balance rather than slaughter bugs.

Plant juice extract is being successfully used against the Japanese beetle, which is good news for most gardeners in the East. Now the bad news—it doesn't work on grapes or roses. Also, the plant used is the exotic neem tree of India, unavailable in the United States. But it really works. The beetles chose to starve to death rather than eat their usual diet when it was sprayed with neem extract. Until we find neem extract at our garden centers, there may be plants in our neighborhood that repel these voracious bugs. We have not yet tried pine extract on beetles, but a New Zealand report says that some pines there contain substances toxic to houseflies, codling moth and apple moth. We intend to try both pine needle and tulip leaf extract on several pests this summer, plus other leaves or weeds that insects never seem to touch.

Mrs. Hedy Reiter of Oliver, British Columbia, finds an efficient plant extract in her garbage. She saves all her citrus and banana peels and lets them soak in a two-gallon pail for several days. "This gives you a strong tea which turns the bugs down the road," she says. "I use an old paintbrush to sprinkle the tea,

These Colorado potato beetles are easy to collect. With small insects, you may be able to collect only a spoonful. If so, the method still may work.

dipping it into the liquid and swinging it over the rows of plants to douse them evenly." The spent peels are placed under the plants. In midsummer, she gathers alfalfa and clover, adding a clove or two of garlic, and uses the mixture "on everything." Most garden pests do indeed leave these field legumes alone, and Mrs. Reiter is undoubtedly on to something.

The idea of using a pest against itself ("Everything contains the seed of its own destruction," said Ms. Bubb in her first letter to us) has been given a new wrinkle at the University of Kentucky, where Dr. Joseph Kuc has been vaccinating plants against virulent fungus diseases. He weakens the fungi and sprays them on plants, which respond by forming sticky substances to hold the spores in clumps on the leaf surfaces. The plants can then produce antibodies against the fungus. He's grown several squash and melon varieties successfully after directly contaminating the leaves with plant disease.

As we study the bug juice and plant juice methods more thoroughly, we'll be able to be more specific about what works. In the meantime, be a blender spray pioneer. You have nothing to lose but your pest problems.

THE BUG JUICE METHOD

Determine which pest is causing, or about to cause, damage to your crop. Collect as many of the offenders as you can without exceeding a half cup. Place the bugs in a blender with two cups of water and whiz until homogenized. Strain. *Use all of it right away or freeze the remainder.* The only possible danger with this method is to let the bug juice sit out and become contaminated with salmonella bacteria as it decays. There's no danger if it's used within an hour or two, or the unused portion is frozen. Since the extract can be diluted up to 25,000 times, it's a good idea to freeze some for reapplication after a rain. We are still learning, so please let us know if it works. Do not use this method on any pests of man—houseflies, mosquitoes, fleas, ticks—as they may harbor human diseases.

THE PLANT JUICE METHOD

Find a nonpoisonous weed or tree leaves that are seldom bothered by insects. Whiz a couple of handfuls in the blender with water, strain, and spray on the crop being damaged. Dilute no more than five times. Select smooth-leaved plants, as these are unpalatable to insects because of some substance in the leaves. Hairy-leaved plants repel insects mechanically. You are, in effect, making your crop unpalatable to bugs. Choose plants like pine, poplar or herbs that you know are nonpoisonous, yet contain volatile oils.

JEFF COX

FALL-PLANTED POTATOES – THE EASY WAY TO EARLIER HARVESTS

Why store seed potatoes in the house when they winter over under garden mulch?

HAVE YOU ever considered the advantages of planting your potatoes or purchased seed potatoes in the fall?

You don't have to live south of the Mason-Dixon line to plant spuds in the fall. Think back to past years. Have you missed potatoes while harvesting them only to discover them as green plants the following spring? It tells you at least one of two things. The first is that potatoes can be successfully planted in the fall in your area. The other is that you might be a little set in your ways.

The advantages in planting potatoes in the fall go beyond solving immediate storage problems. Potatoes grow best under cold-weather conditions. The earlier they are planted, the longer your cold growing season will be. Spuds grown during cold weather are more resistant to blight. And fall is the earliest you can get your seed potatoes underground.

Think cool and the final result will be quality. "Cool" spuds have class. When cooked, they have more body. This quality has been attributed to the retention of starch during cool nights. Having them planted before the season begins insures the maximum amount of cold growing. If Mother Nature works her miracles on schedule, you should be having your early potatoes steamed and buttered with your peas.

If you wait until the ground thaws in the spring, the soil will be too wet and compact when worked. Potatoes need loose soil for air. Fall planting permits working the soil at your convenience. Having pleasant working conditions should inspire you to be more thorough in your soil preparation, a must with potatoes.

Potatoes demand well-aerated soil. This can be achieved by tilling or disking after plowing. Spading will suffice if you dig deep and break up the clods. Adding compost increases the organic content of the soil and allows air spaces to improve tilth. Beware of fresh manure when working with potatoes. Planting in the fall

118

would give it some time to decompose but it increases the acidity of the soil, inviting scab. What benefits tubers most is potash. Before putting your seed potatoes to rest for the winter, work greensand, granite dust, ground potash, or powdered feldspar into the soil.

Potatoes thrive in loamy, somewhat sandy soil. Clay lacks air while retaining water. This is particularly bad when considering planting in the fall. When the water in the clay freezes, so will your seed potatoes.

Plan your garden location so that you will not be planting in an area where you have grown potatoes, tomatoes, eggplant, peppers, or petunias. These plants are related and invite soil deficiencies. Crops to follow in the same plot would be beans, peas or Japanese millet. Soybeans work miracles in refreshing the soil. To improve the flavor of potatoes, plant sets in last season's nasturtium bed.

Plant varieties which do well in your geographical zone. Seed catalogs are virtual encyclopedias for information on zones as well as the varieties available. Keep in mind that the earlier varieties are more blight resistant. Examples would be KENNEBEC, ANOKA, and PONTIAC REDS. For extra vitamin C content, WHITE COBBLER and KATAHDIN would be good choices. Good keepers include NORGOLD RUSSETT.

Although seed potatoes are in abundance in the fall, they may not be available where you shop. A seed catalog is the best answer. Buying potatoes from the grocery store and hoping they will suffice is risky. You may get a variety that doesn't do well in your area, and they could carry disease. When buying for seed, always make sure they are certified disease-free. Disease can decimate your harvest and contaminate your potato-growing soil. When using your own potatoes for seed, check them for disease. Infected areas will look like a bruise. When cut, they show a darkened section. It is best to burn diseased potatoes with your trash. Diseased spores can be carried by the wind to parts of your garden if you just toss the unwanted spuds aside. Avoid putting them in your compost pile.

Plant only mature potatoes. You can judge this by rubbing your thumb over the skin. If it rolls back easily, the potato is a bud and not a spud. Use small potatoes as a time-saver. The resulting plant doesn't produce equally small potatoes. The hereditary characteristics are carried by the eye of the potato. When using large potatoes, you must cut them to not more than three eyes per chunk. Too many eyes will try to produce individual plants, which will compete for soil nutrients and result in small potatoes. However, allow enough potato chunk to feed the developing eye. If you must choose between too many eyes or not enough chunk, cut away extra eyes. Cure the cut potato by exposing it to air at least 24 hours to seal the outside.

Plant the seed potato about 4 to 6 inches deep. If you don't have furrows in your worked soil, you can use a bulb planter. Nothing beats the old potato planter, but these are expensive. Space the potatoes about 12 to 15 inches apart. The distance between the rows will be determined by whether or not you plan to do any cultivating by machine. Cultivating and hoeing add air to the soil. However, if your garden has been fed organic matter, air should be plentiful. Machine-cultivate rows 36 inches apart. Hoed gardens use 24-inch spacing.

Fall planted potatoes need about 15 inches of mulch. This can be either straw or hay. If you are concerned with hayseed, buy hay or use some that has been rained on or raked several times. Raking shakes seeds loose.

When spring arrives, you will have your potatoes planted. The storage bins won't need cleaning. You'll not have eaten your seed potatoes and you'll have potatoes on the way.

JEWELL HELQUIST

ALFALFA'S
AMAZING ABILITIES

Don't think alfalfa is for farmers only. It just may be the greatest garden plant ever.

LET ME introduce a plant you're familiar with, and which you think may be quite ordinary—alfalfa. Yet when grown in the garden, it pulls nitrogen from the air and feeds it to soil bacteria, enriching the earth even more than manure. It produces prodigious amounts of humus. It's the perfect mulch. It makes the most superior compost. It's the ideal animal feed. And most amazing of all, we've found that tiny amounts have a growth-stimulating effect that boosts yields of a wide range of garden vegetables.

The source of this effect is a substance called triacontanol.

After the oil crisis in the early 1970's, Dr. Stanley K. Ries, a horticulturist at Michigan State University, began experimenting with nitrogen-rich forages as a fertilizer substitute. The results of his 1975 field trials were puzzling, in that some of the alfalfa-treated plots greatly outyielded chemically fertilized plots. The increases were far above what the nitrogen in the alfalfa could be expected to produce.

In the laboratory they isolated the active agent— triacontanol, a fatty acid alcohol which occurs naturally in the waxy surfaces of the plant's leaves. Additional testing has revealed that triacontanol is not a fertilizer, but a growth-stimulating substance. The less triacontanol you use, the better the results. For example, the most effective application rate of pure triacontanol, Dr. Ries found, is five milligrams mixed with 30 to 40 gallons of water per acre. At that rate, one pound of triacontanol would treat 90,000 acres, and if ready-mixed with water, would take 450 railroad cars to transport.

Dr. Ries has searched for an explanation of why triacontanol works—but the answer has proven to be elusive. In fact, pinning down rates and methods of application has proven almost impossible. All he knows for certain is that the substance has a beneficial effect on such crops as navy beans, asparagus, field corn, sweet corn, carrots, cucumbers, lettuce, radishes and wheat. Other researchers are testing other crops.

At the Organic Gardening Research Center we decided to test the use of greenchop alfalfa in extremely small amounts to see if we could get responses similar to those Ries got using both greenchop and a synthesized form of triacontanol. We were surprised when we found that, indeed, homeopathic doses of greenchop alfalfa produce greater yields than much higher rates.

The greenchop alfalfa was applied before planting at 40, 100 and 1,000 pounds per acre. It was broadcast over the test plots and worked into the soil with a hand tiller. Cucumbers were planted from seed and tomatoes from transplants. The three rates and a check plot were replicated three times, and the smallest amount of alfalfa outyielded the others every time, for both crops (see chart).

The less alfalfa we applied, the better the yield. However, with no alfalfa, we got the lowest yield. The lowest rate we applied, 40 pounds to the acre, works out to just about 1½ ounces of alfalfa for 100 square feet of garden, about one cup of fresh alfalfa. We simply spread the cup of chopped alfalfa over the plot, worked it in, and planted. All plots were mulched with rye straw to keep down weeds.

Before triacontanol becomes something for use in all home gardens, methods of application and rates of application for such small amounts will have to be found. In our trials next year, we will be testing placing individual pieces of alfalfa with transplants, and other methods of applying minute amounts.

If a way can be found to regularly duplicate the 40 percent yield increases Ries has had, the backyard alfalfa patch will surely become a needed part of every garden.

What exactly is this marvelous plant we thought we knew, and what else can it do? Well, it's a perennial herbaceous legume, meaning it can overwinter, doesn't produce woody tissue, and has the power to take nitrogen from the air and add it to the soil. Plants have purple or yellow flowers, with leaves in clusters of threes, on alternate sides of the stem. The plant starts from a crown at or near the surface of the soil, from which five to 25 stems may grow.

Each plant is independent, and although usually thought of as a grass, alfalfa is more like a bush. Left uncut, a plant will reach as much as four to six feet high, with a thick stem. Its botanical name is *Medicago sativa;* its closest relatives are clover, peas and beans.

Alfalfa originated in Southwest Asia, and was grown in Babylon, Persia, Greece and Rome. Its seed was carried to Europe and Spain, on to South America, and finally to California. Europeans refer to alfalfa as lucerne, while North Americans prefer to call it alfalfa, Arabic for "best fodder."

As a pasture crop, alfalfa had no peer when established in the

TRIACONTANOL RESULTS

Tomatoes

Amount Applied — Pounds (per acre)	40	100	1000	None
Tons Per Hectare Yield	84.715	70.410	72.220	67.236

Cucumbers

Amount Applied — Pounds (per acre)	40	100	1000	None
Tons Per Hectare Yield	54.767	53.869	33.476	34.156

The smallest amount of greenchop alfalfa gives the largest yield. Larger amounts of alfalfa show its value as a mulch, but note yield decreases.

Western states in the early 1800's. In the Eastern states it did not do as well, because of sour soils, until liming began. Then alfalfa took off and became the number one forage crop in the country.

The main advantage of alfalfa is its ability to "grow" nitrogren and produce a high-protein forage. As a nitrogen-fixing legume, alfalfa is the standard by which other legumes are compared. Under field conditions, a good stand of alfalfa can fix an average of 300 pounds of nitrogen per acre, per year, by supporting bacteria of the rhizobia family on its root hairs. As the bacteria grow, they take nitrogen from the air and convert it into a solid form. The plant produces a tissue which surrounds the bacteria, forming nodules ranging in size from no bigger than a pinhead to the size of a BB. The plant uses the nitrogen produced by the bacteria, and in exchange provides sugars that the bacteria need to live. When the plant is killed, the nitrogen in the nodules and the extensive root system remain in the soil for future use.

Although many types of rhizobia are present in garden soil, you should expose alfalfa seed to the bacteria before planting to ensure maximum nitrogen fixation. Legume inoculants are sold in garden and feed stores. To check for nitrogen fixation, pull up a plant and cut open a nodule. The pinker it is, the more nitrogen it is producing.

Dr. Donald K. Barnes, a geneticist with the USDA's alfalfa research group, notes that the nitrogen-fixing ability of alfalfa is an inherited trait, and that we can breed varieties for increased nitrogen fixation. In some test plots, they have already found varieties that fix as much as 530 pounds of nitrogen per acre per year. "In the future we will have strains of alfalfa that will fix far more nitrogen than current varieties," he said. When these new varieties are available, you will actually be able to buy a variety of alfalfa designed solely for its fertilizing value.

The top parts of alfalfa also offer your garden a storehouse of nitrogen. In fact, fresh-cut alfalfa contains more nitrogen than any manure. When cut during early bloom, alfalfa will contain just under 20 percent protein. This gives the tops of the plant anywhere from 2.7 to 3.4 percent nitrogen.

In a good year, you can take four cuttings of alfalfa for use as manure in the garden or compost pile. When you turn under a stand of alfalfa, you release the nitrogen in the roots to your soil. The roots of alfalfa will contain anywhere from 1.6 to 2.3 percent nitrogen, less than the tops, but the plant has more tissue underground than it does aboveground. The older the plant, the more total nitrogen and humus you will be adding to your soil.

Dr. Carrol P. Vance, a plant physiologist with the alfalfa research group, recommends that for maximum nitrogen production you take two or three cuttings from a newly established stand before turning it under. A good practice is to take a last cutting just before the first killing frost of fall. Make sure this cutting is as low to the ground as you can get to promote winterkill of the plants, which makes it easier to turn them under the coming spring. If you want to plant as soon as you can in the spring, turn the alfalfa stand under in the fall, top growth and all.

The main ways to use alfalfa in the garden are as a soil-enricher to be rotated through the garden, or as a patch to produce a high-nitrogen material for mulch.

For those who don't have animals, or a neighbor with a well-aged pile of manure to give away, finding nitrogen-containing materials for your compost pile can be a problem.

Alfalfa, however, will provide all the energy your compost pile needs to really heat up and get cooking. Put about a six-inch layer of fresh-cut alfalfa on your compost pile for every foot of garden debris you add, and you'll have it heated up in no time. Be sure to add some good garden soil to get a mix of microbiological life throughout the pile.

If you've got enough nitrogen-rich material for your compost pile, you can use alfalfa as a mulch for all garden plants. At the Organic Gardening and Farming Research Center, almost all of our research plots are mulched with fresh greenchop alfalfa. Not only does it do a very good job of holding down weeds, but it acts as a slow-release fertilizer throughout the year.

Last year we monitored several plantings to test the results of alfalfa mulch. In every case, vegetables mulched with fresh-cut alfalfa outyielded those mulched with black plastic, and weed control was equal. To apply the mulch, plants were transplanted into the field, with a six-to-eight-inch covering around the seedlings. This later settled down to a two-to-three-inch covering around each plant. We used fresh alfalfa from the first cutting of the year, because the timing was right for both transplanting and cutting. For winter vegetables, later cuts of alfalfa could be used.

We also tested the advantage of tilling an area before planting compared to just digging a planting hole in untilled ground. The testing was done in an existing red clover field and a mixed lawn. In the tilled plot, a rotary tiller was run over the area, loosening the soil and incorporating the existing growth. Black plastic or alfalfa mulch was spread and transplants put in. For the untilled tests, a four-inch-square plug of turf was removed and the transplant was planted and mulched.

In the lawn area, the tilled and untilled alfalfa-mulched plots yielded a combined total of 218 pounds of tomatoes, while the black plastic mulch only yielded 159 pounds of tomatoes. In the red clover field, the alfalfa outyielded the plastic mulch, 335 pounds to 305 pounds. The clover outyielded the lawn, only because there were more plants included in that test.

The beauty of using a fertilizing mulch that you can grow yourself should be self-evident. All you have to do is plant a patch of alfalfa, and whenever it starts to bloom, run your mower through it and collect the cuttings. Use these cuttings for your mulch. Not only won't you have weed problems, you also won't have to worry about a midseason feeding, for as the alfalfa mulch breaks down, it will be releasing nitrogen and other nutrients to the plants.

There are two basic ways to use alfalfa in your garden. The ideal way is to plant a part of your garden into alfalfa each year. Take cuttings from the alfalfa to use in the rest of your garden. In the fall, turn the plot under. The next year it will be a well-fertilized area for vegetables. Another area of the garden would be planted to alfalfa the next year. If you devoted one-sixth of your garden to such a practice each year, all parts of the garden would receive a yearly treatment of mulch, and every six years the entire garden would have been green manured.

The combination of a heavily seeded alfalfa crop and regular close cuttings will also give you good weed control. When cutting alfalfa, always cut it as close to the ground as you can. This will not hurt the alfalfa, but will greatly damage weeds. The alfalfa will then regrow ahead of the weeds and shade them out.

The other garden option is to plant a separate area of your property to a fertilizer patch. You can leave an established alfalfa stand alone for a number of years. Some well-established alfalfa pastures have produced good yields for more than 10 years with very little renovation work. If you are growing a patch for the removal of cut alfalfa, it is a good practice to let the first spring cutting lay in the field every year as a mulch and fertilizer. Most years you will be able to remove 3 more cuttings from your patch.

Putting in an alfalfa patch is a great way to reduce the amount of lawn you have to cut. It turns a liability into an asset. All it takes to grow alfalfa is a well-drained, deep soil with a pH of about 7.0. Areas east of the Mississippi normally should be limed for good growth. Potassium and phosphorus usually have to be added when the plot is established, and about every three years thereafter with regular cuttings. Leaving a cutting as a mulch every year will reduce this need. It is not advisable to apply nitrogen to alfalfa, especially when getting a stand established, as the alfalfa doesn't need the nitrogen, and it only spurs weed growth.

For information on varieties and planting dates for alfalfa in your area, contact your local Extension agent. Farmers will also know the planting dates, approximate cutting dates, and the best varieties for your area, as well as sources for seed.

RAY WOLF

GET YOUR SEEDLINGS OFF TO A BETTER START WITH WONDER WATER

Degassed water promises to be a significant aid in sprouting and starting seedlings.

WHEN WE REPORTED in January of 1979 that two Russian scientists had found a sort of "wonder water" that stimulated biological activity, hundreds of readers took up our challenge to test it in their own homes. Researchers at universities and at our Organic Gardening and Farming Research Center also tested it.

Many of those tests are in, and the report is that *Wonder Water works!*

Experiments around the country showed that water boiled for five minutes to drive off dissolved gases, then placed in airtight jars to prevent air from redissolving into the water, had a significantly positive effect on the growth of several vegetables, especially on sugars, lignin and protein that make up the dry matter of plants.

At Tennessee Tech, J. D. Slabaugh, a student working with Assistant Professor Paul Eberhardt in the Plant and Soil Science Department, checked the effect of Wonder Water on tomato seedlings. Slabaugh noticed that "root growth was significantly greater in the plants treated with deoxygenated water than in controls. The more highly developed root systems probably did much to account for the greater development and leaf production of the treated plants and their greater overall vigor."

In Slabaugh's test, Wonder Water tomatoes were taller, had more leaves and nodes, had almost twice as much dry matter and had *two and a half times* the dry root weight of plants watered with ordinary water.

We also checked the effects of Wonder Water on tomatoes and lettuce, among other plants, at our Research Center in Maxatawny, Pennsylvania. Although our results were inconclusive (an infestation of whitefly in the greenhouse during the test introduced a variable that may have skewed the results), the figures were promising. The lettuce results were interesting—the Wonder Water plants were the smallest, yet when dried and weighed, they contained more dry matter. We'll be taking another look at Wonder Water in fall.

Wonder Water's greater biological activity was noticed by Shannon Southerland of Blountville, Tennessee, who sent us this report: "This is my first year in gardening, and naturally I chose the organic method. I decided to experiment with Wonder Water after reading your article, so I degassed a quart of tap water and soaked some seeds in it. I soaked some others in plain tap water. The results were great. In several days, five Wonder Water seeds had sprouted, with rootlets about half an inch long. The ones in tap water weren't doing half as well—only two had sprouted and they'd barely emerged. Then I decided to go further with the experiment.

"I planted three seeds soaked in degassed water, three seeds soaked in tap water and three seeds not soaked at all. A week later all three Wonder Water seeds had come up and were an inch or more tall. The ones I had soaked in tap water were barely breaking the ground, and the ones I didn't soak at all weren't even up yet. Since the results were so good, I plan on soaking all my seeds in degassed water before I plant them."

Myron Hartz's ecology class at a Norfolk, Virginia, junior high school tried Wonder Water as a class project. They soaked beans in tap water and in Wonder Water. The first group of 60 beans was soaked for 96 hours and weighed. The average weight gain per tap water bean was 4.24 grams, while for the Wonder Water beans it was 4.75 grams. A second group of 70 beans was soaked for 48 hours, half in tap and half in degassed water. The tap water beans had gained an average of 3.88 grams, while the Wonder Water beans gained an average of 4.11 grams. "The difference may not be significant," Hartz says. Since the Wonder Water beans averaged about 10 percent more than the others, we'd say it's significant.

James Stewart, working in State College, Pennsylvania, experimented with bush beans and Wonder Water. He soaked some beans in Wonder Water, some in tap water, for 11 days. At the end of that time, the Wonder Water beans were out-sprouting the others, but it was immediately apparent that the degassed water had a terrific effect on the beans' rootlet formation. Of the 15 tap water beans, 14 had no rootlets, while one bean had four. In the degassed sample, five beans had no rootlets, two had three rootlets, four had four, two had five, and one bean had six rootlets!

Fred Ponting of Red Bluff, California, tried the experiment on soybeans, alfalfa seeds and mung beans. To sum up, the Wonder

Water soybeans germinated better and grew longer rootlets than tap water beans. "Ninety-eight hours into the test, the degassed water beans were plumper, more succulent, and had a cleaner appearance. Tap water beans were shriveled at their tips and seemed to have degraded in quality," he reports. He estimated that the Wonder Water beans weighed 15 percent more than the tap water beans.

In his alfalfa test, Ponting says that "72 hours into the test, it was obvious the Wonder Water sprouts were ahead at least 20 percent by bulk due to longer, plumper, more thrifty sprouts, and from better germination. The quality and appearance were better by a marked degree." The mung bean test showed no advantage for Wonder Water beans. He tried the mung beans again with the same results.

Danny Wallace of the University of Missouri College of Agriculture did what appears to be the most thorough test. He used peas, soaking and growing them to maturity using three types of water—a control, a frozen-thawed water (which is degassed but not as completely as boiled water) and Wonder Water. He studied comparative amounts of final top growth, final root growth, total wet weight, total dry weight, flowering and podding rate, and the final number of pods. Looking more closely at the pods, he studied pod wet weight, pod dry weight, and the number of seeds in each pod.

"The results of the experiment were remarkable," Danny wrote in his final research paper. The Wonder Water group of peas showed 49 percent greater fresh growth, 59 *percent greater dry weight, and twice as many seeds per pod* as the ordinary water control. The experiment was much more complex and scientifically rigorous than we have space for here, but the results moved Danny to this conclusion, which goes for us, too:

"The phenomenon of Wonder Water is very new to science. Someday, when it's put to large-scale use, it will have an amazing impact on agriculture. Who knows? Maybe the use of Wonder Water will be a major instrument in curbing the shortage of food."

JEFF COX

HOW TO MAKE AND USE
WONDER WATER

RUSSIAN SCIENTISTS discovered Wonder Water by accident, but soon were reporting its ability to increase biological activity. From the reports we've received, and from our own studies, we think the results show that seeds benefit when soaked in Wonder Water, and seedlings benefit when watered with it. They appear to grow thriftier, with better root branching and earlier, stronger germination. The benefits for houseplants are obvious, too.

Step One   Secure as many glass canning jars, lids and rings as you want to make quarts of Wonder Water.

Step Two   Bring that many quarts of water to a rolling boil and allow to boil for five minutes. This brings dissolved gasses in the water as low as a half-part per million, which is very effective.

Step Three   Heat the jars under the hot water spigot to prevent cracking when the boiling water is poured into them. Fill each right to the top with boiling water, put on the lid and screw it down tight so there is very little or no air inside.

Step Four   Allow the jars to cool by setting them on the counter. The water will remain degassed until the jars are opened and exposed to air.

When using Wonder Water for houseplants, seed-soaking, sprouting or watering seedlings (and maybe taking a drink yourself), use each jar right away. Once opened, gasses immediately start to redissolve in the water, so it can't be used again. When pouring the water, try to avoid letting it splash and bubble, as it may quickly recapture gasses.

WUNDERKIND WINS WITH WONDER WATER

I SHOULD HAVE written much sooner. I'm 12 years old, going into seventh grade this winter. We had a Science Fair last school year. You know what a Science Fair is—where you try out new things to see if they work.

I tried out Wonder Water on some beans. I got one box and filled it with dirt, and planted the beans. This box of beans I watered with regular water. I called them the "control group." I did the same with another box, but watered it with Wonder Water. They were entered in the Science Fair and I got *First Place!*

The seeds in the control group didn't do well, but the ones in the Wonder Water group did fine. Operation "Wonder Water" proved a success!!

YOUR GARDENER,
ELAINE RHEA RICHARDSON
HAMILTON, MISSOURI